A TEENAGER'S JOURNEY

Also by Richard B. Pelzer

A Brother's Journey

A TEENAGER'S JOURNEY

Overcoming a Childhood of Abuse

Richard B. Pelzer

WARNER WELLNESS

NEW YORK   BOSTON

Warner Wellness

Warner Books
Time Warner Book Group
1271 Avenue of the Americas, New York, NY 10020
Visit our Web site at www.twbookmark.com.

Warner Wellness and the Warner Wellness logo
are trademarks of Time Warner Book Group Inc.

First published in Great Britain by Time Warner Books in 2006

Printed in the United States of America

First Edition: May 2006
10 9 8 7 6 5 4 3 2 1

Library of Congress Control Number: 2005937641

Book design by Charles Sutherland

*This book is dedicated to my children.
The teenage years are the hardest, but can also be the most
rewarding. May you learn not only from what I have been
through, but also from what no young adult
should ever have to go through.
I will always be there for each of you.
Love,
Dad*

ACKNOWLEDGMENTS

This work would not have been possible without the tenderness and patience of my wife Joanne. Special thanks to Mr. and Mrs. Digby Diehl, my editor Barbara Daniel, my agent Jim Schiavone, Ron Goodson, Chris and Geoffrey Tubbs, and Judy Prince-Hansen. And of course the Nichols family, thank you all.

CONTENTS

INTRODUCTION

In order for you, the reader, to understand and appreciate what this book means to me, I must provide some insight as to what my life was like prior to my teen years.

We were to all appearances a normal middle-class family in a small city just outside San Francisco, California, called Daly City. With most families in the neighborhood, at least one of the parents worked a middle-class job. My father was no different.

He worked as a fireman in San Francisco. Mom stayed home and took care of the five boys. On the surface, there was nothing out of the ordinary about us. We were just like the rest—at least, up to the point where I became aware that what happened to us as boys at home was different than what other children experienced in the neighborhood—or the country, for that matter.

We lived like wolves, able to turn on one another at will, able to devour one another when need be. It was necessary.

However perverted it may sound, it was nothing less than a matter of survival.

In the early days, I don't think any of us kids felt that what was happening was "over the top." It was all we knew. Perhaps my older brothers knew better, perhaps they experienced similar things before I came along. I don't know. I can only speculate about what happened before I was born.

From my earliest memories, life was completely and utterly bizarre. Inside the house and with the protection of privacy, Mom's ability to demonize and control her children knew no bounds. Eventually she mastered the ability to terrify a child beyond mortal horror. For many adults, it's traumatic to have to come to terms with your own mortality. But when a child becomes conscious of walking a tightrope between life and death, the struggle to survive becomes personal, a matter of endurance; much like a pro athlete pushing himself beyond what he thinks he is capable of just so as to push himself even further. When a child has to constantly endure in order to survive, each accomplishment, each victory no matter how small, gives him the willpower to continue and endure even more.

For me, by the time I reached fifteen, I'd found other ways to endure: alcohol and drugs. It wasn't as if I was the only teen who drank in my school—most of the kids I knew drank. Most of the kids I hung out with did an assortment of drugs: nothing outrageous—marijuana, speed, crystal methamphetamine, cocaine, or the occasional hallucinogenic.

Alcohol was different. At first it was a matter of desire: a desire to get drunk. Later it was more of a need to get completely bombed. As I look back now, I know the answer to the question most kids asked me: why I liked hard liquor when the rest preferred beer. It was just part of my personality. From drinking to drugs, everything I did had to be harder, bigger, more dangerous than what those around me were doing. As a teenager, I had an addictive and dangerous personality. It was much as I'd been as a child. In fact, it was a tribute to my childhood.

I started drinking at the age of fifteen. I never liked the taste of beer—it always filled me up and I found it difficult to drink fast. On the routine errands that Mom sent me on to the local liquor store, with a note to the store clerk giving me permission to buy a pack of cigarettes for her, I usually managed to leave with a pack or two of smokes and a bottle of bourbon or vodka for myself. And no, the note said nothing about permission to steal—I authorized that on my own. Self-sanctioned destruction. That's what most of my young adult life was like.

As I turned sixteen, the realization that I was nearly six feet tall and weighed almost one hundred and eighty pounds spared me from any further physical abuse at the hands of my mother. But it meant an intensification of the mental and emotional abuse, which was actually more damaging to me than being beaten unconscious or deprived of sleep for days.

As a teenager, I often wished Mom would make me sit on the hardwood floor again with my hands folded together, knuckles down. The pain of my own weight crushing my hands as I sat on them for hours was not as bad as feeling the eyes of the neighbors on me as I walked past their houses, knowing that Mom had probably regaled each one of them many times with accounts of my faults as a teen. Usually she would get the name of the drug or the brand of booze wrong, as she magnified my misdemeanors to any neighbor or stranger who happened to pick up the phone when she called. I always felt as if every one of the neighbors and even people several streets over knew my every move. It was shameful to feel their piercing stares and their complete disgust as they looked at me. Mom made no secret of who she called and when she called them. The only thing she kept to herself was the neighbors' eventual pleas for her to stop. Mom not only embarrassed me at my expense, she also embarrassed herself at my expense. There was no limit to what she would do to ensure I continued to feel less than human.

At first I always drank with at least one other teen, or a few friends. We hung out in the woods behind a small group of apartments just down the street. There we shared many "firsts": a first kiss, a first smoke, a first hit off a joint, and even the first sexual experience. But with the move from my hometown in California to a new town, Sandy City, Utah, came my introduction to solitude. I knew no one, no one my age who drank or smoked or did drugs. Sandy City and most of Salt Lake City, most of the state for that matter, was very religious.

It took me several weeks to find the few fellow students who lived as I did: a life of drinking and drug abuse, secretive and out of control. By that time I preferred to drink alone, anyhow. I enjoyed the local park after dark, long after closing. I spent more time alone, after midnight, drinking myself into the Stone Age at Mesa Park than I spent sitting in class at Hillcrest High School.

The world was changing all around me, but everything I did and everyone I came across seemed meaningless and impersonal: everyone except Darlene. At that point, Darlene was the only one who could reach me. She was the only one that even tried. She introduced me to her husband, her family, and a few select neighbors, including Judy Prince—people who weren't tainted by Mom's negative influence—not yet, anyway.

Looking back, I know that her kindness, her love, and her unsolicited recognition saved me. What Darlene gave me at that time was more than I had ever expected from anyone. What she gave I treasured above everything.

She gave me respect, and the opportunity to speak.

She gave me friendship.

She gave me hope.

From the day I met Darlene my life changed—for the better, but also for the worse.

Now I was exposed to what a real family had to do to function. I was totally confused: my need and my overpowering desire to destroy myself conflicted with the love and respect I was being so freely given.

As a teenager, I made a lot of mistakes and some very poor choices that could have affected me for the rest of my life. Luckily, only a few of those mistakes have dogged my adult life. I could have been so much worse off than I am. I also know that there are teens today who are worse off than I ever was: more self-destructive, more ashamed, more hurtful, and more dangerous.

I also know why.

There are events in life that we have to experience for ourselves: our first love, the birth of a first child, the loss of a loved one. There are other lessons that we can learn through other people's experiences. Those lessons spare us the cost and pain of personal experience. They also provide us with insight.

That's the reason this book has been published: to give all of us an understanding of just what a teenager, pushed to extremes, will do and how desperate he or she can become in the search for love and *self.*

I survived one of the most horrific and abusive childhoods imaginable. Those few people who knew what was happening did nothing to help. They were afraid to.

I was confused and I was damaged. My entire teenage life I continued the self-destruction. It became part of me. It constituted who I was and what I thought about myself.

This experience has helped me in ways that few people will ever understand. Until now.

A TEENAGER'S JOURNEY

1

GOOD-BYE, CALIFORNIA

I had been part of what can only have been one of the worst instances of child abuse in America of the 1970s. But the preteen that once held me captive was gone—I was a teenager, and I was different now. I was determined to either stand up for myself or give up.

Unfortunately I chose to give up. I wanted, needed, to take my own life.

MORNING CAME, AND I leapt out of bed and got dressed before anyone was up. For the first time in years, I was happy. The rest of the household were going to be away for two weeks. I was finally going to be alone.

A few nights before, I had been in the basement, reflecting on my life—on the child I had been and the events that had shaped who I had become. The basement had always been a place I wished I could forget. Its concrete walls held all the emotions, fears, and tears of the little boys—me and my brother David—captured and forced down there and abused. Those concrete walls held the secrets that only a few knew about. It was as if the emotions that had been absorbed in the concrete were what held the foundations together.

The memories of the things that had happened in the basement terrified me. They were telling me something, and I couldn't make sense of what I thought I remembered. I recalled myself as a little boy hiding in the basement from Mom, like an animal. Months before, the hamster that lived in my room had escaped and found his way down to the basement. I found him hiding and shaking with fear under the steps. The same hiding place I knew so well. The memory of Mom laughing as she left me cowering under the metal shelves that had fallen on top of me once she'd shoved me into them—the debris crushing me and her laughter as she walked away hurt me more deeply than I can put words to.

That's what most of my late childhood and young teenage life was like. I struggled to find words that described how I felt. I had outgrown my stuttering. I was older now. Instead of words getting tangled in my throat I found it hard to find words that expressed the hurt, the anger, and the shame.

When I recalled that same little boy slumped on the bottom step, staring at a pool of my own blood after Mom had thrown me to the concrete floor, smashing my head, I saw my face reflected: meeker than meek and utterly humiliated. I was so ashamed of what I was as a child. The ghost of my past, the memories of the child who had been so abused, haunted me. Often those apparitions would reappear in my dreams, but that one night, a few nights before, the ghosts were telling me to accept the fact that I was no longer that scared little boy.

As I got older, and felt I understood something about what had been happening to me, to an extent I was able to let go of it. But those experiences had not disappeared. Much like many apparitions will do, they reappeared when I least expected it.

Now I was a teenager, and one thing I did know: I'd seen more misery than any child should have to, and I wanted it all to end. I wanted the shame to go away, the fear to evaporate, and mostly, I wanted the ghosts of my past to just leave me alone. I wanted, needed, to end my life.

———

After Dad's death, Mom and Scott, my older brother, had decided to sell the house in Daly City, California, and move to Salt Lake City, Utah. The house was worth twenty-five times what Mom and Dad had paid for it years before.

When she left me in Daly City that morning, while she and "her family" went on their two-week vacation to look for a new house in Salt Lake, Mom made it a point that I "might not" be moving there with them. On the one hand I was relieved to be left alone. On the other I had no idea how or where I would live if they did leave me behind. I desperately wanted to leave that house and all the memories that lived there. I also knew that being fifteen and homeless in San Francisco was a frightening notion.

I guess what eased the fear was the belief that even if I was homeless, I would be better off. Meanwhile, I was determined to make the most of my temporary respite, no matter how short-lived it was.

———————————

Two weeks later, they were back. Mom and I were in the kitchen and she was doing her best, as usual, to degrade me. Only this time, she was ranting worse than normal. For hours I'd been listening to her drunken lies and delusions. She was pushing me further and further; her constant bombardment of insults was building up inside of me.

While they'd been away, I'd spent some of the money she'd left for me on new clothes. I'd been wearing the same shirt and pants for a year. It had felt so awesome going to JCPenney and buying myself new clothes. I knew she'd be mad if she found out, so I'd stuffed all the packaging into the garbage cans before they got back from Salt Lake that night. What I failed to anticipate was that she would go through the cans and find everything I'd put there. Not only the clothing packaging, but soda cans, and even the take-out container from lunch the day before. She was furious with me.

Suddenly, out of pure anger at what she was saying and doing to me, I made my hand into a fist and was about to square up to her. That rage helped me forgive myself for having been so timid up till then. I welcomed it, and yet I was afraid of it: that pure wrath, that building anger. I was terrified of the volcano nearing eruption from deep inside me. I knew that if I ever allowed that volcano to erupt, if I ever let go, it would be bad: really bad.

I backed down. I had to. I knew she was over the edge. It was three fifteen in the morning. Obediently, I picked up the trash she'd emptied out onto the dining-room table, cleaned up the floor, and went to bed.

The next morning, I dressed, went quietly into the dining room, and found the sugar bowl in the china cabinet. There I had placed most of my earnings from my paper routes. I took out all the cash. It amounted to just over fifty dollars.

I was disappointed that there was only fifty left, and I knew that the money I had hidden in the bottom of my dresser drawer was long gone. I had been spending more and more on whatever drugs I could find.

At first I'd taken on one paper route as a means of not only getting out of the house, but as a way of putting a few bucks in my pocket. Once I learned how expensive my new fondness for pot and cocaine had become, I had to take on a second, then a third paper route. The more I earned, the more I was spending. I was always broke, and yet wanting, needing, more cocaine. It was a vicious circle, and there was only one way to break it—I took on several more paper routes. In the weeks before we left Daly City Mom's threat to leave me behind had come to nothing. I was delivering three free papers to over thirty streets in my neighborhood. I also was responsible for several other routes delivering different papers that covered the same area. Each week nearly three thousand newspapers, all told, were being dropped in my driveway in bundles of fifty.

Not a single paper ever made it to any of the houses on my routes. At first I would dump them in the open sewer drain at the end of Crestline Avenue near the bottom of Westmore Hill. That disposal site worked well enough until I realized that it was backing up after heavy rains. The next site I found was a little more convenient, but more risky.

I placed the bundles behind the front steps of the house of a neighbor who recycled papers to raise funds for the local scouts. Thanks to the recycling center and to this neighbor who, like the rest, willingly turned a blind eye to the fact that so many papers were turning up for recycling, this went on for some time. Eventually, though, it became too risky. He asked me to no longer drop them off at his house, as he was having to explain how he came by prebundled newspapers, papers that looked like they had never been unbun-dled, let alone read by anyone.

The next disposal site was the best. It was convenient and well hidden. Soon after the truck left my driveway each Monday, Wednesday, Friday, and Saturday at 2 A.M., I would take the bundles to the trees behind the apartments where I hung out during the day. The papers provided warmth when burned, as well as seats to place neatly around the makeshift campfire my friends and I had built deep in the woods.

Many nights I spent sitting with a few friends, from well after midnight to dawn, smoking joints and drinking bour-bon at that simple homemade campsite. As I took on more and more paper routes I spent more and more time in the woods behind the apartment complex near the end of Crest-line Avenue. At first it was almost every night. I was sad-dened when fewer and fewer friends were able to spend the entire night out. Before we left Daly City I was spending most nights in the woods at "Camp Paper," and that's when I realized that my preference was for drinking alone. More times than not I was alone in the woods. Just me and Jim Beam, my new best friend, and my small campfire; although he didn't share anything of any value with me, my new best friend gave me more comfort than even Josh used to do. (Josh lived across the street, and had been my best friend since elementary school.)

Sad as it is to admit, being alone in the woods with a small fire to keep me warm, plus whatever it was that Jim Beam put in those dark square bottles, kept me together, mentally and emotionally. By now I was making nearly three hundred dollars a week not delivering newspapers. Almost all of it went up in smoke, up my nose, or down my throat.

Whenever Mom drove me and my brother Scott down to the Crocker National Bank near Serramonte shopping center I'd shake my head in disbelief. My brother would cash one or two checks while I would be cashing over a dozen. Mom never said a word—she never asked nor did she even care. She had no idea I was not delivering on all those routes. She assumed I was slow at delivering the one or two she knew of. And most of the time she never cared, either, that I was out of the house nearly all night most of the school week.

The only time she would have a word to say about it was when I was still asleep when the truck honked after dropping off another load in the driveway; then she would yell for me to get out of bed and deliver those papers.

As I reached into the sugar bowl I knew there wouldn't be much left. I had been using the money on booze and drugs almost as fast as I wasn't earning it.

Finding just slightly more than I needed for the gun was a relief.

As I stuffed the bills in my pocket, I looked down the hallway to Mom's room and smiled.

I'm going to beat you at your own game, I told her silently.

I turned around and walked out the front door. The normal walk to my old elementary school took about forty-five minutes. This time I wasn't going there, but to a friend's house just past the school yard. I didn't have many friends—I only knew a couple of boys about my age who didn't make fun of me or treat me poorly. They simply accepted me.

Jonathan was just such a friend. In the classroom, where other kids would tease me about the way I looked or smelled or about the clothes I had on, Jonathan would somehow make me feel better. He was smaller than I was and was picked on for different reasons. Together we sort of kept each other's spirits up.

He was one of the few people I had confided in other than my best friend Josh. He knew about Mom, how she beat me and how she constantly made me feel less than human. Jonathan couldn't truly know how bad it was, yet he understood. Our conversations were short and usually started with him asking what had been happening to me, especially if I looked more tired than usual.

He had offered to sell me a gun if I ever wanted to stop Mom. At the time I thought about it, but I'd never had the guts to seriously consider actually killing anyone—until now.

As I walked the same streets that led me both to school and toward Jonathan's house, I thought about why I was so comfortable with the idea of suicide. Ever since that night in the basement when I'd thought so much about my life and even seemed to have made some sense of it, I had been determined to end it one way or another. All I had to do was find a way. I knew my friend was serious about the gun. As I made my way along the path through the trees by Westmore Hill, I realized that I wasn't scared; I was comfortable.

Before long I made it to Jonathan's house. I rang the doorbell, knowing in my heart that everything would be all right. His father answered the door, and I asked if his son was able to speak to me. He invited me into the house, and Jonathan came into the hallway and motioned for me to follow him downstairs.

In the corner of the basement was a small cabinet with a few pistols and rifles.

"If your dad finds out, there'll be serious trouble," I said.

"I've done it before," he replied smugly.

He had little concern about selling one of his father's guns without his knowledge. I knew that someday his father would discover it missing, but I wasn't going to be around to learn of the outcome.

He took out what looked like a chrome-plated thirty-caliber automatic handgun. Without hesitating, I handed him the agreed forty dollars. My friend unloaded the magazine from the handle and showed me the several rounds, then reloaded the magazine. I thought to myself: *All I needed was one bullet, but it doesn't matter.*

I stuffed the pistol in my pocket and we left the basement via the garage door. I said good-bye and walked down the street. I could feel the weight of the gun in my pocket. It gave me satisfaction.

The walk back to the house I called "home" was almost spiritual. I took notice of the tree paths and the streets leading up to Westmore Hill. *I will never see them again*, I thought. At the steps to the high school I sat down, feeling the cold stone. I thought back to the house, and the basement. I was happy inside. For the first time in years I really felt happy.

I found my favorite place among the trees where I would often go and talk with God. I'd been talking to God for a while now, but it was always a one-sided conversation. I felt this would probably be my last talk with him. As I pondered taking my own life, the feeling came over me that if I did I would in some way be offending him. I wasn't sure why, but it seemed as if I would be giving up, and in an odd sort of way, giving in.

So, if I do this what will happen to me? I asked God.

As I lay on my back talking to him, I realized that the decision to take my life was all my own. God would have nothing to do with a teenager committing suicide.

I know I've been a disappointment to you and I know that you're angry with me. I just can't do this anymore, I respectfully and sincerely said. *If you're going to help me then help me now!*

As the last words softly left my lips I waited anxiously for a response. The minutes passed and the anxiety became anger as I realized that I wasn't getting any answers.

Eventually I gave up and found comfort in the thought that I was once again on my own. I started to think about how and where I would do it. The thought of the gun firing and the impact of a bullet to the head made me wonder just how fast death would come.

What if it isn't as quick as I think it will be?

What if I can feel the bullet rush through my skull tearing the bone apart, scattering it everywhere?

As I pondered my fear of the unknown, I realized that there was just no way of knowing what to expect.

It's not like I can ask someone who's done it, I thought.

I sat and pondered some more, this time about when I learned that my neighbor down the street had jumped off the Golden Gate Bridge. She worked for the local phone company. When I was eight or nine years old, I used to secretly spend time talking to her when Mom was too busy with other things. As I thought about that day, I recalled the emotions that her mother shared with me: The sheer sense of emptiness and wonderment was overpowering. I kept wondering what could have caused her to actually go through with it. She was a pretty girl who seemed to have friends. I didn't know what was on her mind or what was lacking in her life, but I knew that she felt strongly about it. She must have had a good reason. I recalled the few ink portraits I made. She had introduced me to a whole new form of speech by teaching me how to take ink to canvas and how to use pictures and not words to express myself. I wondered where they were now.

I knew that I would never know the reason why she did it, and I felt empty inside. The only people I would want to understand, when I was truly ready to do the same, were my two brothers Ross and Keith. They were the only ones that would even care, the only ones that would miss me.

Once I realized that there would be no answers to my questions in my conversation with God, I felt a sense of sorrow.

Please, please help me.

I don't know what to do.

I'm afraid. I'm lost.

Why are you letting me do this? I cried.

The next few minutes ticked by so slowly. A part of me wanted some sort of divine intervention, yet another part of me wanted confirmation that my decision to take my life was the right one. Neither came as I lay on my back looking at the clouds passing overhead.

Well then, I have nothing to lose, I said.

I stood up and looked back. I could see the tree line and the trails made by the hundreds of us kids as we all walked the same path to school each day. I recalled the years before when I would wander the school grounds looking for an answer, the hours and hours I'd spent sitting in the school bathrooms crying.

All I want is for someone to love me, I thought, as I started to make my way back home.

A few yards farther on I found another place to sit and mull things over. I recalled better times, me sitting on Mom's lap being comforted when I had a fever or banged my knee as a little child—I knew that she was capable of love.

But that was back then, before David left. David was older than me; he was born after Ross, my favorite brother, and before Scott. For as long as I could remember, David had taken the brunt of Mom's venom. He lived in the basement. Often when Mom referred to him she called him "It." Mom made him work till he dropped, and most of the time past that point. She beat him daily, kicked him, cut him, and starved him. More than once she locked him in the bathroom with a pail of cleaning solutions mixed together to make a toxic gas. She made him eat out of the dog dish under the kitchen table when the rest of the "family" ate in the dining room.

Then when he was thirteen or so, he disappeared. I thought at first that Mom had finally killed him; perhaps he'd failed to do something she'd told him to do. I was terrified. If she actually killed him, who else might she kill? It took me a while to learn that he was actually rescued and that the police had taken him away.

One thing I had known. I'd just felt it and it was as real as those apparitions in the basement that night: Mom needed a victim, and I'd be the next one. It hadn't taken long for my feelings to turn into a frightening reality.

On the one hand, I hated her with every ounce of my body and wished her dead more times than I could count. On the other, I remembered the times I'd wanted her never to leave me, to protect me from all the bad things the world had shown me. In a way I felt sorry for her and wished that I could erase all the pain and embarrassment she must feel inside from the guilt of the horrors she'd committed. I often wondered whether, if I told her I was the reason that she was abusive, perhaps she would let it all go and return to being the "Mommy" I longed for.

I thought about the big dinners she would serve and the games of Tripoli we used to play in earlier years, and the comfort we'd all felt. Trying to make sense of it all was near impossible. When I was small she could comfort me as a mother, while at the same time committing acts against my brother that bordered on attempted murder. That much I understood. She was simply not in control of her actions or her thoughts. I believed that at times she had different personalities. Looking back at my childhood and all the times that I thought were good, those same times when David was going through hell, what was so strange was the realization that *she was the same person.* She could comfort me while beating him senseless.

I became convinced that she had lost her mind and was truly sick. In an odd sort of way that knowledge comforted me. The understanding gave me satisfaction, some sort of answer.

With a feeling of strength renewed, I stood up and continued on my way back home. Once I turned the corner onto Crestline Avenue, I saw the house—that dismal, dark, cold house. As I got closer and closer to the front steps I became ever more determined to find the perfect moment and place to take my life. My decision was made. I had no reason to postpone it any longer. I didn't want to just struggle on and on, endlessly questioning myself. I just wanted it over with.

Confidently, I walked quietly up the steps and into the front room. Everyone was still asleep. I made it back in time, before anyone had even noticed that I was gone.

Once in my room, I walked over to the black desk and sat down. Through the window, I looked at Josh's house across the street and knew that within a few short hours I would either be on my way to Salt Lake City or in the morgue. Perhaps at last I would be somewhere I would be loved. A place where I could find the answers to the questions I had asked myself so many times as I lay on my back talking to no one—perhaps now I would find out if there was a God or not. I looked forward to the answers. But I struggled with the question of the exact time and place. Where? When? Before everyone got in the car for the ride to Salt Lake City? Perhaps I could do it in the backyard. I had thought about doing it in the backyard for a while now. It seemed almost the right place. Or I could wait until I was in the car and we were all together.

But by now the removal men had pulled into the driveway and started to load what belongings we had already boxed up. Mom and Scott were packing the car. Once they were done, the neighbors came out one by one and said their good-byes. They all had kept silent about what they had seen and heard in our house. I watched them, and I shook my head sadly. I was more than disappointed—every one of them had known what was going on and yet not one had stood up to help us.

———————

Had this been 2006 and not 1980, anyone in the neighborhood, any of the teachers or administrators, any adult who had known what was happening in that house, would have stood up and helped me and my brothers. We have come a long way in twenty-five years. No one with a heart can stand on the sidelines and allow the kind of horrible abuse that existed in that house for so many years. Today, anyone knowing of such horror, such evil, would be held accountable. They would find themselves having to answer for their silence.

———————

Frank and Alice from next door came out and hugged each of us, then talked to Mom for a few minutes. I looked Frank and Alice in the face and sensed they genuinely felt guilty. Helen, the neighbor on the opposite side, came out, too, and said her good-byes. Even my older friend, Ben, who lived just down the street, hugged me and rubbed my hair as he often did to say good-bye. The last to show themselves were Josh and his family. They all came out and hugged each of us. Then Josh and I sat on the curb and talked about writing to each other. Josh had been my best friend all along. I was happy being around him and I'd enjoyed his friendship.

In a dead serious but gentle tone, I told Josh that I wouldn't be able to write back.

"I am going to end this nightmare once and for all," I said, as I patted the pocket that held my pistol.

Josh had seen Mom beat me and he'd seen Mom embarrass me more times than I could count. Even when I was running away from her, mortified with shame, and Josh was standing there watching in horror, he was always my friend. For years he had seen what I had gone through and tried not to make a big deal about it when I was so ashamed.

One of the more difficult and awkward situations I experienced was when Josh and I were freshmen in the same class at Westmore High School. It had to do with my smoking, which I had managed to keep hidden from Josh and his family for a couple of years. I was able to get away with smoking at school by keeping my cigarettes tucked into the top of my sock.

In the middle of class one day Josh turned to me and asked: "Did you drop these?"

"Yeah—thanks," I replied, as he handed me the pack. It had somehow fallen to the floor as Josh sat down in front of me.

He was obviously mad at me. He had commented several times how he hated the way my mom smoked and smelled of cigarettes. Having handed me the pack, he simply turned away and ignored me for the rest of the class.

I felt both embarrassed and relieved. I was sad that he'd found out I was smoking by some simple accident rather than me talking to him about it. But I was relieved that I'd only dropped the cigarettes and nothing else.

As I casually slipped them back into the top of my sock I leaned toward my other leg to check that I hadn't also dropped what was hidden there. I was relieved to discover the couple of joints and the small bag of cocaine I had stowed there.

I knew if Josh had ever found out I was doing drugs he would have written me off and never talked to me again. *Thank God*, I thought as I sat back in my chair and continued to ignore the teacher and everything else that was going on around me.

As we sat there on the curb outside the house in those few moments before I would leave and never see him again, Josh turned and looked at me. His face told me that he understood. He reached out and put his arm around my shoulder. I held back my tears. I was feeling the loss of a true friendship, and I knew he felt the same. But now I was being instructed to get in the backseat of our new car. Once Mom was in, we backed out of the driveway and turned down Crestline Avenue for the last time. I sat up and watched Josh out the back window as he waved good-bye. Once the car turned off the street Josh, Ben, and all the others were out of sight.

As I turned back into my seat I looked at Mom, and she glanced back at me. *If you only knew what you've done to me,* I said to myself as she turned back to her driving. I placed my hand over my pocket, felt the pistol, leaned back, and closed my eyes.

All I need now is the perfect place and time, I thought to myself as I drifted off.

I felt in my heart that soon enough I would be where I'd wanted to be all along: a place where I would be safe and warm, a place where I was loved, a place called heaven, a place I could really call home.

2

THE ANGEL

There was nothing that impressed me as a teenager. I found little pleasure or happiness in anything I experienced. But then I saw the angel, and I was deeply touched. I found myself questioning my decision to take my own life. There was just such a peace about the face of the angel that I was no longer sure about my decision, or about anything else.

WE WERE LEAVING THE Daly City area. I watched the landmarks pass by as we drove farther and farther out of California. When we crossed the Golden Gate Bridge for the last time, I recalled the fun we'd had as boys marveling at its height and size. That was long before Mom had changed into the person I now feared. And I thought of my friend who had found the courage to jump from the very edifice we were now crossing.

Once we reached the Oakland side, we were on the open road and well on the way to the Promised Land of Salt Lake

City, Utah. We had been traveling for several hours and I was drifting in and out of sleep. Scott was driving. Just outside the California-Nevada border, we stopped at a small-town hotel casino. My younger brother Keith and I wanted to stretch our legs. We got out of the car and started to walk around, looking at the huge signs surrounding the casino.

"Richard, get back in the car—*now!*" Mom yelled across the parking lot. Halfway back to the car, I noticed that Keith hadn't turned around to walk back with me. Then I saw him—Keith, Scott, and Mom were making their way toward the building. I watched as they went inside.

Back in the car, I felt that familiar feeling—separated, singled out.

Whatever! It won't be long now, I said to myself.

As I sat there enjoying the morning sunlight, they returned with a few souvenirs from the casino and some drinks for each of them. Mom brought nothing for me.

Once we were back on the road I kept myself occupied by daydreaming, again, about the time and place I would select to take my life. The hours passed. We made one stop after another to stretch our legs, and I became engrossed with the countryside: We were entering the Nevada Desert. What seemed like hundreds of miles of blacktop highway kept the ride quiet and I slept for most of the drive. I heard Mom talking to Scott and Keith. They would stop at the salt flats and Dinosaur Land, she said, where the kids could see real dinosaur bones just as they had been excavated.

One of the few photos I have of Mom was taken at Dinosaur Land. I'm not sure who took it, or why I ever held on to it. It was a good reminder of just who she was, certainly. I always thought it appropriate that one of the few photos I have of her shows her with gigantic, vicious carnivores towering above her.

Scott walked on ahead around the outside of the park, while Mom followed, holding Keith's hand. She would occasionally stop, then catch up with Scott. It never concerned her that I was often out of her sight. Whenever I had the chance, which was most of the time, I would set off in the opposite direction from Mom and "her boys." Whenever I saw them together, I felt excluded. Mom was very careful to make sure that I knew there were two parts to her family: "her boys," and me.

As the distance between us lengthened, I passed the entrance to what seemed like a small enclosure. Off to the left were some bat caves. Before anyone could notice, I slipped into the crowd and joined the short tour in the caves.

We went deeper and deeper into the caves. It was getting darker and damper all the time. When we were right inside, far enough in to embrace the darkness completely, we were all asked to be as silent as possible and to listen and watch for the animals flying around the roof. Before long, I could see and hear the bats. Some hung on the ceiling, silent. I was amazed at the numbers of them, and at the dampness in the cave. The dark and the damp felt familiar.

As I walked out of the cave and back to the exit of the enclosure, I was struck by the scenery. The desert was dotted for what seemed like miles around with small islands of trees and plants. I leaned against the wooden fence and surveyed the vast landscape.

"What the hell do you think you're doing?" she said.

I knew the voice, and I loathed the tone; I didn't look back to check that it was Mom, I knew it was. I straightened up from the fence, hung my head, and awaited her instructions.

"Get back there, behind Keith!" she commanded.

As I skirted her and Scott, then fell in behind Keith, I could see the stuffed animal he was carrying. She must have taken them inside the park and spent some "quality time" with her boys.

As we walked back toward the parking lot, I told Keith about the bat cave I had found. Within a moment he had informed Mom of it, and without hesitating she turned around and made directly for the cave entrance. As she purchased the tickets for the tour, I knew she would exclude me. Sure enough, she handed Scott and Keith their tickets and told me to wait by the fence where I had been when she found me.

"The tour is for me and my boys—not you," she said.

Finally she's leaving me in peace! I said to myself as I fixed my gaze on the view I'd found so interesting just a few minutes before. A short time later, Mom returned with the boys and led us back to the car.

———

Just inside Utah, we came to the Bonneville Salt Flats. It was our first real stop where I'd really be able to roam around. Ironically, there was nothing there. The miles and miles of flat, tightly packed salt reminded me of the emptiness and solitude I had become so accustomed to: apparently strong, yet fragile—much like me at the time.

We went for a short trip to Old Salt-Air Park. Mom said it was one of the best amusement parks she could remember. She used to go there as a child with Gram and ride on the carousel and be treated to candy, she told the boys. It was almost as if she had found a pleasant memory, and it was one of the few times I recall her talking about her own mother without exploding in a fit of vulgarity. There weren't many times that I recalled Mom talking about her childhood and saying something nice about it.

Then we made it out to the site where the rest stop at the Old Salt-Air Park once stood. It used to be a proud building, Mom said. Now it was nothing more than an unkempt tourist site. Like most others did, we stayed a few minutes, then drove on. It was almost comforting to see one of her childhood memories reduced to rubble. In my own twisted way, I took pride in the fact that she was disappointed.

The ride from there to the new house was only a few more hours. Now inside Salt Lake City, we were driving down one of the main streets, just behind Temple Square. A left turn, and we were headed up to the avenues and into an old cemetery. As Scott drove, Mom kept on about this large stone angel—a landmark that would lead her to the graves she was looking for. Scott was becoming frustrated, as she ranted on about this angel. Then I saw it. Near the top of one of the long avenues that dissected the cemetery and off to the left a bit, near the middle of the rows of graves, stood a large stone angel. We parked and made our way toward it, but then Mom veered off in a different direction, Scott and Keith trailing behind her as she talked.

Quietly I walked up to the still, silent statue and marveled at the detail and the beauty of it. I had no idea whose grave it marked or what it symbolized. But I knew that someone must have felt very special about the person buried there. I looked closer and read what was written on it: A child was buried beneath the stone. She had a simple, pretty name and had died at a young age. The words told of the love that one mother could have for her child.

I was frozen with wonder, and at the same time elated to see the grave in all its glory. The angel's face was emotionless and her pose was restful, almost as if she was happy to be there, at that moment in time. And for that moment I, too, was glad to be there. I had seen something that I knew I would remember till the day I died. I felt a quiet and a calmness in my heart. It seemed in no way odd that I found comfort among the headstones and the graves.

As I stood in front of the angel, I looked into her face and saw there an expression of joy and peace. I must have stood there all of twenty minutes before I finally walked away. I looked over toward Mom and the boys, and it struck me that perhaps my idea of committing suicide was wrong. There was something about the angel that kept me thinking I had made a wrong decision.

I made my way back to the boys. Mom was telling them of family members who were buried in the cemetery. As I approached, she stopped short and ordered me back to the car. I felt somehow comfortable as I passed by the angel again, and rubbed my hand on the cold stone. As I did so, I whispered: *Thank you.*

3

WHERE TO NOW?

*One of the most important conversations I had with God
occurred at the very moment I reached in my pocket for the
gun. I wasn't scared, I wasn't afraid—I was simply lost.*

*Mom had led the neighbors and anyone else that would
listen to believe that I was dangerous and mentally unstable. I was certainly losing the little stability I had. I was desperate. I learned later that some of the answers I had been
looking for were in the silence I heard as I waited for God's
response to my pleas for help.*

THE DRIVE TO SANDY CITY, UTAH, from
downtown Salt Lake was short. Within a few minutes
we were driving down 13th East, looking for Mulberry Way.
Not far into the subdistrict was our new home. We pulled
into the driveway, and Scott immediately opened the two-
car garage and the door to the backyard. He made it a point
to let me know what the garage was for.

"Our cars," he said.

"You don't have a car," I replied.

"Mom's buying me one," he smirked.

We walked through the garage and into the downstairs. The first room we passed on the left was our oldest brother Ross's room, Keith told me. It was by far the largest room in the house, and Ross had been gone for well over a year now. He was in the services somewhere inside the U.S.—I didn't know where. He'd made it out of the house of madness, and he wasn't coming back. I was sure that the furthest thing from his mind was any thought of coming "home"—to the old house, the new house, to the old town or the new one; it was all the same—insane.

At the end of the hall was a half-open door, displaying old orange and red shag carpet. It screamed of the 1970s and reeked of urine and mold. I stuck my head into the room and looked around. Scott had come down the steps to where I was now standing. "That's yours and this one is mine," he informed me, pointing to the next bedroom.

"It doesn't matter," I said, as I went in and closed the door behind me.

I opened the window that led directly to the backyard. Looking around, I saw that one of the baseboard panels was hanging off the wall. I'd discovered the perfect hiding place for the gun. I carefully lifted the panel, took the gun from my pocket, and placed it on the cement floor inside the small space, then covered it with the baseboard. Once I was sure I was alone, I felt for the top of the sock on my right foot and found the few hits of acid-laced postage stamps I had left.

I let the stamp dissolve on my tongue, waiting for the almost spiritual hallucinations I was more than used to on my frequent acid trips.

Before long we'd had the furniture delivered and installed in our rooms. I spent some time out of sight, in my room, organizing what little furniture of mine had made the trip. It didn't take long—all I had was a twin bed and a coffee table. There was no closet to place what clothes I had, so I simply laid them out on the table and went upstairs to find Keith. Keith's room was next to Mom's, and about the same size as mine.

The next few days were spent unpacking and settling in. The time passed quickly. After dinner each evening I went to my room and lay on my bed thinking about what I was going to do.

I'm not sure I can actually go through with it, I thought to myself one night as I drifted off to sleep.

At some point in the night I awoke—to silence. I was sure that I had heard something, though, and had been woken by the noise. Cringing, I expected the door to my room to open and to see Mom standing there. But it was the newness of the room and the unfamiliarity of the house that had startled me. Within a few short minutes I realized that there was no one there, and that I was safe.

Over the next few nights the same silence woke me over and over again. It was as if I was supposed to be awake and expecting something to happen. It wasn't long before I realized what was breaking my sleep: it was the habit I had formed as a safeguard when Mom would come into my room at the house in Daly City.

In my old room I kept several large objects I had collected from the neighborhood trash. They were a safety mechanism—nothing more. Placed carefully in the center of the room, they allowed me time to escape from Mom. Each morning she would chase me around the house before school to punish me for what I was going to do wrong that day. The furniture and other heaped-up items allowed me a brief opportunity to gain time on Mom as she pursued me. Once I was close enough to the front door I could usually make it outside to the front yard, then run for school. Occasionally, I made it out of the house without a beating.

It was becoming annoying. Odd as it may sound, the silence was still waking me. Pondering what to do, I wandered upstairs and looked around the living room. It was at the front of the house and had a large window that looked directly onto the street. I felt about in the darkness, and found a wooden rocking chair off to the left. I sat down. I hadn't noticed it before, and couldn't place it in the old house. I just couldn't recall Mom ever having had a rocking chair. Bewildered, I sat and wondered what else I hadn't noticed. Across from the window, in front of the TV, was a recliner. Something else I hadn't registered in the old house.

Sitting in the rocking chair, looking out the window, I resumed my ongoing conversation with God. Before I spoke, I cleared my thoughts and looked for that feeling of warmth and comfort.

Please, please, just take my life and bring me home. I'm afraid to do it myself. I just can't stand my life any longer. I'm begging you!

It was as sincere and honest a prayer as I had ever offered. Sitting there awaiting a response, I actually felt that this time I would finally receive an answer, that I was about to leave my miserable life behind. A feeling came over me that I can only describe as calmness; I was comfortable with the thought that I was about to receive an answer. I sat in that chair for over an hour, waiting. As the time passed, I began to doubt those previous feelings of comfort and wondered if I was simply wasting my time again. I began an inventory of all the other times I'd believed that God was listening and that I was being heard—and I realized, again, that I was alone.

When I opened my eyes I saw that dawn was nearing, and I would have to return to my room. Thinking about the room, I could envision myself lying on the bed, stoned out of my mind. I felt like a vampire that roams the night and must return to the safety of darkness and the sanctity of drugs. I had to return to the darkness of my room before it was noticed that I wasn't there.

I lay awake and wondered what I had to do to be acknowledged by God.

What am I not doing? Why am I alone in this? I asked him.

Before long the sounds of the day were pressing in on me, and I was told to go and clean the garage and help sort it out. I dressed, then went to the garage, where I found stacks and stacks of boxes heaped all over the floor. Mom and Scott were already working on them. I'd hardly made my way up the steps when Scott announced: "You should be doing this, and *we* should be out buying my car."

Without acknowledging him, I walked over near Mom and awaited my instructions. As I expected, I was asked to stack boxes along the far wall, the ones that Scott and Mom had already gone through as they determined what needed to be unpacked and what didn't. I felt really angry when I saw Mom looking through a box that contained a few of the small items I'd had in my old room.

"Put this on the bottom of the stack—over there," she commanded, promptly closing the box when she realized I'd seen what it contained, just those few mementoes from what seemed like a lifetime ago.

By dinnertime, the work was nearly done. All the while Scott and Mom kept up a conversation about the things they wanted to buy and the furniture they needed to replace.

At one point I joined in, and asked: "Will I be able to get those eyeglasses now?"

I had been after Mom for over a year to get a pair of glasses. I could barely see the blackboard—or anything at all farther away than ten feet—but as always, Mom shrugged it off as "unnecessary."

This time she never even gave me the satisfaction of another refusal. They both just continued their conversation, not even acknowledging that I had interrupted them. I didn't really expect her to allow me to have them, and truly I didn't care; I knew I wasn't going to be around much longer anyway.

Once the garage was fairly organized, we quit for the day and ordered out for pizza. After dinner I went back to my room and took an inventory of my thoughts, my feelings, and myself. Would I ever stop being miserable at simply being alive? Lying on my bed, I glanced over at the baseboard where I had hid the gun, and retrieved it. Placing it under my pillow I calmly said: *That's it—I'm done.*

I was tired of being left hanging, tired of being who I was, and most of all just tired.

Shortly after dark I had awoken once again to the silence in my room. I reached my hand under the pillow and felt the cold of the gunmetal. I pulled out the gun, looked it over, released the magazine from the handle. Looking into the clip, I saw that there were several rounds. Then I placed the magazine back in the handle, released the slide back in place, loading one round in the chamber.

Confidently, I walked out of my room and up the steps to the living room. As I passed by, I saw that Scott and Mom were watching TV. Moving out onto the deck just off the kitchen, I noticed the small bench surrounding the tree in the center of the backyard, and sat down on it.

Well, I guess this is as good a place as any, I thought.

Reaching my hand over my pants pocket, I felt the metal and wondered: *What will they do when they hear the shot? Will they even look in the backyard to see what it is?*

Who cares! I said to myself.

Was I really about to remove the gun from my pocket? I'd resolved that once I did that, I'd use it as quickly as possible.

I didn't want to think about it or wonder about it anymore. I just wanted to be able to actually do it. I closed my eyes—and froze. For a moment I wanted to hold on and see if this last chance at being heard by God might come to something. Secretly, I wanted God to send an angel down to stop me—*some* kind of intervention, anything. I kept my eyes closed and listened to the silence that filled the backyard.

Within a moment I knew that I wasn't going to get any response.

I quickly pulled the pistol out of my pocket and put the barrel to my temple. I recalled the many hours I'd spent debating with myself how the shot would sound, the impact of the bullet, and whether the possibility that I would screw it up and live was worth the risk.

When I'd finally decided that it was more than worth it, I felt at ease with myself. It was almost as if I had control over the situation and no one else could change it or take it away from me.

I tried not to pause as I put my finger through the trigger guard and felt the cold metal. I closed my eyes tighter and squeezed. I started to shake.

In that moment I experienced an understanding of time itself. In what took only a fragment of a moment, I experienced the passing of time like I never had before. After what seemed like minutes, I wondered if I had done it and it was already over. Perhaps I was already dead and I just didn't realize it.

My hope that it was much easier than I had imagined was a warm and welcome thought. Slowly, I opened my eyes, fearful of what I was about to see and experience, knowing I was dead.

In an instant I realized I was still right where I was a moment ago and that the safety guard had not been removed when I squeezed the trigger.

Damn it!

"God damn it!" I said.

I had to do it all again—and quickly, before I lost the courage. Then it happened . . .

. . . "Richard, get up here, there's someone here to see you," Mom called down to me as I sat on the bench.

For a moment I held on to the darkness that filled my eyes, then closed them again. I lowered the gun from my head and felt the back of my hand hit the wood railing of the bench. Every ounce of energy I had was gone; every spark of life inside me was gone. In that moment I felt I had lost what little I had left of myself. I was truly empty—absent of any emotion, feeling, concern, or fear.

I sat for another moment, absorbing the fact that I couldn't even take my own life—not with a gun. The only emotion I could feel surfacing was shame.

I stood up and went quickly up the back steps. A neighbor had come down the street from her house to welcome us into the neighborhood.

As I listened to her and Mom talk about where we came from and what ages we boys were, I faded in and out of listening. I looked down over the rail of the porch at the bench I had been sitting on only a few moments before.

Now the woman came over to me and introduced herself as Darlene Nichols. She lived up the street with her husband

John and their children Wendy, Steve, Heidi, and Heather. By now Mom and Scott had disappeared into the kitchen. Within a few minutes Darlene had managed to capture my attention and was talking to me on the back deck.

Her demeanor was so sincere and her voice was so genuine that I was absolutely captured by her presence. She told me of several teenagers in the neighborhood about my age who would be happy to show me around and invite me to outings and sports events, if I was interested. Darlene looked at her watch, saw that it was getting late, and asked if I wanted to meet her husband the next morning. We had been talking for well over an hour.

I was so overcome that someone so kind and polite would take such an interest in me, I forgot about the earlier moments in the backyard sitting on the bench around the tree with the gun in my pocket. All I could do was respond: "Sure!"

I had found in my heart something I had never felt before. It was a quiet calmness—almost as if I was asleep. I found that I was contemplating "tomorrow." If I would just make the short walk up the street to their house, perhaps I could postpone my plans for a while. I was confused—I didn't really know what to do. Moments before Darlene had introduced herself to me I was that close to suicide, and now I was looking forward to being introduced to the rest of the Nichols family. It was hopeful in the sense that I had a chance to find teens my own age, and yet it was annoying that something else had interrupted my plan to take my own life.

———————

I walked Darlene to the front door, thanked her, and said good night. I paused as I closed the door, then went down to my room, unnoticed.

Sitting on the edge of the bed, I felt the gun in my pocket and pulled it out.

Maybe this can wait for another day, I said to myself.

I placed the gun back into its hiding place behind the baseboard and went to bed. As I drifted off to sleep I wrestled with the idea that perhaps, I had received my answer.

It can't be that it's that simple. There's no way that I was that close and all it took was someone new showing up at the house.

As I closed my eyes I felt a sense of gratitude and said softly: "*Thank you. Thank you.*"

4

SPEAK NO EVIL

John and Darlene were real. The way they lived, loved, and honored life was so foreign to me. The distance between what they knew about me and the secrets I kept inside was infinite. I knew they would never believe a word of it. I thought about it a few times and what, if anything, I could say to John and Darlene or even if I could ask for their help. It didn't take me long to realize that they would not want me around them or their children if they knew I was as angry at the world as I was. There was just no way I could expect them to understand or believe that I was living with one of the most abusive parents—if not the most—in the state of California's history.

It was hard to accept the fact that they wouldn't have believed any of it.

EARLY THE NEXT MORNING, Saturday, I got dressed and made my way up the street looking for the house number that Darlene had given me. When I found it,

I walked around to the side door. A crowd of people were in the backyard, working. I made my way in, and Darlene noticed my arrival straightaway, and welcomed me.

In the yard, a man was laying out pieces of sod. Even though he was kneeling down and facing the opposite direction, I could tell that he was very tall. When Darlene introduced me to John, her husband, he stood up, put his hand out, and welcomed me to the neighborhood. As he stood up, as if in slow motion, I was intimidated to see the sheer size of the man. He seemed larger than life—he was well over six feet tall. I expected a loud and commanding voice, but he was just as gentle as Darlene, and carried himself much the same. His demeanor was sincere and made me feel welcome.

Working with John was a young couple that I was also introduced to, named Kevin and Sandy. They, too, radiated the same sincere and positive outlook. As if all of them together shared some secret to life that made them happy and content—they overwhelmed me.

During the next few weeks, John and Darlene made me feel as if I was a part of their family. I often spent time watching movies with them and the kids; we shared in activities as a group—as a family.

When they asked me to babysit the kids and again share time with them, I was excited by this show of confidence in me. As the summer went on and school returned, I spent more and more of my time after school at the Nichols family home. Mostly, I would hurry home off the school bus and spend as little time there as possible before heading up to their house.

I was secretly comparing myself to Wendy and Steve—the oldest of the Nichols children. I knew that they would never experience an ounce of what I had been through, and what I was hiding. Even though I knew it was almost futile to compare myself to them—I was nearly sixteen and Wendy and Steve were ten and nine years old, respectively—I wanted to understand how they interacted with each other so well.

I recalled myself at nine years old: when I was in the ambulance being rushed to the hospital after one of Mom's explosive beatings, and the times I had spent hiding like an animal in the basement of the house in Daly City.

Neither of them stuttered like I had, and they both enjoyed being around their parents. In fact, Wendy and Steve were so foreign to what I was at that age I just couldn't relate to their outward personalities. They unintentionally intimidated me.

It soon became all too apparent that Mom was getting upset with me as I found happiness with the Nichols family. And it didn't take long before she found a way to intervene. Up till now, Mom had always been very careful to limit interactions between her and me when we were outside the secrecy of the house. But now she knew I was spending as much time away from our house as possible, and she didn't have as much of an opportunity to abuse me, mentally or emotionally.

I had created a sort of routine with John and Darlene. On Friday nights I would make a pizza and bring it over so we all could share and watch a movie. Initially I was stunned by their commitment to their family in only showing appropriate-rated movies for the kids. But as time went on I learned that they had expectations of themselves as well as of their children. I quickly came around and was comfortable with the selections they made—"G" movies, although often boring, were welcome.

On one such Friday, right after I came home from school, Mom made it a point to ensure that I knew she had called the Nichols family. I was "not going to get away with the way I was acting around *her* home and then prance off to the Nichols house and hide!" she had informed them.

I was crushed to learn that she had called Darlene, my Darlene, and embarrassed me. I wasn't sure what she had really said and was hesitant to ask.

As soon as I got to their house, Darlene said: "Cathy called and told us that your behavior with her is terrible." After a moment or two, she asked if Cathy, my mother, drank. She had noticed that during the conversation Mom had sounded as if she had been drinking, but since it was still only early morning, Darlene wasn't sure if it was true.

"She does drink. She drinks a lot," I said.

I felt sure that they would look on Mom's drinking as a reflection on me, and hold me in a different light. But to my amazement and delight both John and Darlene indicated that they'd suspected Mom drank and that there was an "issue" between her and me.

Careful not to interfere, they each tried to deal with Mom and her lifestyle as best they could. Had they known about Mom's schizophrenic behavior, I was sure they would have kept their distance from both her and me.

I knew there was nothing I could ever say that would help them understand. They were safe in their ignorance—ignorant of the facts and the reality of what I was living through. By no means were they lacking intelligence or personality: They were simply so unfamiliar with the physical abuse I had endured as a child and the mental and emotional abuse I was now so used to.

———————

It wasn't long before Mom formed the habit of letting John and Darlene know about every move I made. When I talked back or stood my ground, or when I went and did things that "the Nichols family wouldn't approve of," she made sure they knew about it. She was trying her hardest to place a wedge between me and the family that I had come to respect and love. Eventually, I became embarrassed that she was always calling Darlene, trying her patience. But Darlene was always careful to let Mom know that the Richard she portrayed was not the one that she, Darlene, knew. "I just don't see that behavior in him when he's here," she told Mom.

John and Darlene provided more support and comfort for me in the few short weeks that it took to know them than Mom had done in my whole life. Now, finding little success in her attempts to make me as miserable as she was when I wasn't around her, she started down a new path.

I was well aware of what she had been telling them, but I couldn't believe the tricks she would stoop to. At one point she started to make up stories about these huge verbal fights, and eventually physical fights, we were supposed to be having, and about how abusive I was to *her*. She also fabricated stories to do with my morality, about the sexual antics I was getting up to. Not that I hadn't spent time with girls in secret—and I'd been sneaking them into my room at night— but she wasn't even getting the stories *right*. That's what pissed me off—she wasn't even lying truthfully.

By now, Mom knew that I was drinking, smoking cigarettes, and using drugs. So she would try and make up stories about that, too. But when she exaggerated my drunkenness or the number of times I was strung out, she never got the details quite right. She never got *any* of it right. Yes, I was using, and found comfort in it. My few friends at the high school were users, and it kept us together as a clique.

At first it was simple, it was easy to obtain. The occasional joint between classes would seldom lead to anything else during the school day. As time went on, and Mom became more than an annoyance to the Nichols family, she started to reach out to other neighbors. And the harder she tried to tear my world—such as it was—apart, the bigger and better the drugs I began to find. The more Mom lied about my drug use the more I was determined to prove her right.

Again, what really got to me was her ignorance on the subject. She could never get the story right. When I was using cocaine she would say it was pot. When I went drinking with the few girls I knew in school, she would say that I was stealing her vodka and drinking it myself. Before long, I gave up on explaining to John and Darlene that Mom had no idea what she was talking about. I saw that they were able to figure that out for themselves.

Mom had long ago mastered the ability to make my life miserable and useless. Now my new world had become fragile, translucent. Nothing was kept private. Everything I did was reported and exaggerated. At one point John and Darlene decided that they wouldn't listen to her any longer, but simply allow me to be the person I was now becoming. Since I kept my drinking and drug use to myself, never admitting it to anyone, the Nichols family had no idea that Mom was in some ways right.

I was learning to share in the lives of their kids and see them grow and develop as they went through school and the daily routines of a large family. I learned firsthand about siblings, and the routines they shared. I was learning what "normal" was.

Just before my sixteenth birthday John and Darlene inquired whether I was thinking of getting my driver's license, not knowing that the subject was at the core of many nights of argument between Mom and me. Since I was not yet eighteen, I needed her to sign for a minor's license and, of course, she refused.

Darlene wanted to know why Mom wouldn't allow me to get one. Having no idea that she was falling right into the trap Mom was so used to setting, Darlene called her on the phone to convince her I should have a license. I knew Mom would paint the blackest picture of me possible. And of course I couldn't tell Darlene that even though Mom had the names of the drugs wrong and the brand of liquor wrong, I was very deeply involved in both. I played ignorant and hoped Mom would eventually disgrace herself.

When I walked into the house one afternoon, I heard Mom on the phone talking. I wondered if she was calling the Nichols family again and making me look as bad as usual. Once she noticed I was in the room, she turned abruptly in the other direction and continued: "You just don't know how violent he can be. Putting him behind the wheel of a car is too dangerous. He's always high on something."

I knew who she was talking to, and what she had planned.

This went on for several months. I started to withdraw from the Nichols family, embarrassed over the way Mom was treating them. It came to the point where she would call them more often than she would argue with me. Since I found myself once again caught in one of her devices for keeping me down and depressed, I began to look for another outlet, another way of passing time.

Some of the students at the high school I attended had similar issues at home, and I found a sort of comfort in knowing that I was not the only one in Sandy City, Utah, who lived like this. Many of them looked as if they lived the way I did, surviving from one day to the next. The way they looked, dressed, and spoke, they—like me—stood out from the normal teens chatting and laughing in the hallways.

Other teens in the school knew that the "stoners" were different from the rest of the various cliques. Everyone assumed that all we did was hang out—skip class and drink and use drugs during school. They weren't exactly wrong— they just didn't understand the whys of our situation. I guess each clique made assumptions about what it would be like to be in a different one, but no one ever bothered to ask. Both the students and the staff simply labeled us as "trouble." None of us were *real* trouble; we just had issues that we didn't understand or know how to deal with. We were all just like each other, really. Whether we were "jocks," "geeks," or popular, we were all often confused and insecure—all of us.

Once I started to associate with more of the students, I found myself under difficult social pressures. Before long I was skipping all the classes and going to parties during the day, returning to school just in time to catch the bus home. Several times I tried new drugs and found that I had no idea how to hide what I was doing, or how other teenagers got away with hiding it. Up till then I had thought I knew exactly what I was doing when it came to girls, drugs, and alcohol, but I soon realized I had no idea.

I spent less and less time with the Nichols family, and after a while joined a particular small group of students. One of them, Nathan Bennett, took me under his wing. His father had long since taken off. His mother had become an alcoholic and was barely able to keep the two of them together. Within a few weeks I was familiar with his lifestyle, and more specifically with the effects of various hallucinogenic drugs. I experimented with far more drugs than I had ever done before.

I always had a liking for the combination of cocaine and alcohol. Many times during school I was so tired and so sick that the only way I could function at all was to keep the high going. Thus I was feeding a vicious circle of destruction that would eventually come to a head.

My schoolwork was long past the point of recovery, and this soon became apparent to the school's vice principal. When it became obvious that I was not going to earn enough credits to graduate to my sophomore year, the vice principal called home and informed Mom that I had missed over half of the school year in partial absences. He also told her that I had been sent home several times for smoking behind the gym.

All of this played into Mom's hands—yet another reason to make me look like a seriously troubled loser, not only to the Nichols family but now to the other neighbors that had become friendly to me—Robert and Judy Prince. Rob and Judy lived across the street from the Nichols family, and they, too, had showed an interest in my behavior. Occasionally when I needed to talk to an adult about my issues I would confide in Judy.

This couple, like Darlene and John, allowed me to share in their lives, at the same time attempting to teach me that my current lifestyle left much to be desired. Whenever I needed to talk to someone and was uncomfortable sharing with John and Darlene out of embarrassment, I found that Judy would be able to understand and show that she could still care for my safety and health without demonizing me.

As the school year ended in the summer of 1981, I found that the friendships I thought I had made had evaporated. All that kept us kids together was the constant partying. At the age of seventeen, I felt once again that my life had no direction, that I was caught up in my own vacuum of self-destruction. There became less and less of a need for Mom to exaggerate my flaws—they were becoming more than apparent to those that now knew me. I didn't care anymore what Mom told the neighbors.

I didn't care anymore about anything. I stopped beating myself up over the conflict between trying to be a "good kid" whenever I was around the Nichols or Prince families and the reality of the life I was really living. It used to tear me apart, knowing that I could be exposed at any moment and would have to explain everything to John, Darlene, and Judy. But not any longer. I just didn't care anymore.

Most parents don't understand anything. They never know as much as their own kids and never understand what it is like to be a teenager: Somehow, they forget. Mom was worse than that, with her outrageous stories. But the worst of it was that I found myself living them out. The more outrageous the lie, the more I would turn what she said into the truth. I had become nearly everything she told any neighbor who would listen: a thief, a cheat, a drunk, a drug addict. I was methodically working my way through the mass of names she labeled me with—one at a time.

It gave me security, being one person around some people and someone completely different around others. It gave me power and control over who I was and over what I would do and when. For the first time I was really in control of my life by allowing it to be completely *out* of control. It was all my own doing, and no one could tell me otherwise. No one really knew me—including myself. But this multiple personality became difficult to manage.

By Thanksgiving, I had stolen several gallon bottles of Mom's vodka and had them hidden away for my own use. Within a week the stash that once comprised eight gallons was now reduced to one last bottle. I reconnected with the same friends from last year at school and followed the same patterns as before. I fell back into the void that was the acceptance of my peers and of the girls that associated with us. By now, my morals were just about nonexistent. I became more involved in drugs, alcohol, and girls. I was becoming, just like Mom, horribly miserable.

I found better drugs and better parties. My inexperience with girls was a thing of the past, and I was now just one of the group. I'd spend many afternoons in a girlfriend's bedroom, then off to a party in the early evening. As time went on it became sort of expected that as I showed up with a girl from the pack we would get hazed over what everyone already knew we'd just been doing. It became a contest to see who could "hook up" with the most girls during the year. I had no remorse over the loss of my pride, my morals, or my dignity. We all shared with each other—the same group of guys and girls. When one couple broke up, each would hook up with someone else within the group, even if they had already been an item in the past. I had dated several of the girls more than once.

Like the rest of the group, I was just seeking the comfort of someone to be with, physically.

By Christmas, Mom and I had had several heated arguments over my escalating drug abuse and drinking. She had now started calling Grandma in Holiday, Utah, to let her know that I was serious bad news and that she didn't know what to do. She needed another outlet to reach out to, as the Nichols and Prince families had begun to ignore Mom and her stories about me, whether true or false.

Christmas was both one of the hardest times and the best of times for me as a child. I recall the magic that surrounded Santa, and the traditional Christmas lineup where each of us boys would arrange ourselves by age in the hallway just outside my room for the procession to the front room to view the mounds of toys and other presents that Santa had left each good boy. But as I got older, I remember fewer and fewer gifts for me and even more for the other kids.

One year I learned the reality of Christmas for me. Mom had taken me down to the basement. I had been crying under the Christmas tree, clutching my two comic coloring books—my only gifts from Santa. That Christmas, she made it very clear to me that she was the only reason I even got that much.

I thought back to the wonderment and yet the utter disappointment of those memories. They had all left me behind—Mom, the old neighbors, the old school, the nurses and doctors I'd encountered, even Santa—they all pretended I didn't exist. I promised myself that I would learn from my mistakes, and renewed my vow never to believe in anyone.

Past experiences had taught me that I was better off distancing myself from the family during the festive season.

Oftentimes, during the month of December that year, I would leave the house after dinner and walk up to Mesa Park near the top of the street and sit there for hours. Christmas Eve, I snuck out my bedroom window and found myself at the park well after midnight with another bottle of vodka that I'd stolen from Mom. I sat in the park and drank as much as I could.

Many nights I had slept in the park, and no one ever noticed. I knew when the police cruisers would patrol the area, and I knew when and where to hide.

As I sat and pondered my life, I realized that I was becoming a person I loathed, even more than in earlier years. I was becoming mean and aggressive. I was drunk more often than I was sober, and I knew I was using alcohol as a means of dealing with my lack of self-pride. I was becoming like Mom, and I knew it. The only difference I could see between Mom and me, at that point, was that I used a greater variety of drugs.

By 3 A.M. I'd had more than my fill of vodka, and I was freezing. Thinking about what I was doing, and just the fact of being alone, made me angrier and angrier. The trip back to the house was less than a mile, and I usually made it in about twenty minutes. As I walked down Mulberry Way and past the houses, I took in the Christmas lights and the feelings of the season as the street quietly slept. Stumbling along, I passed Rob and Judy's house and felt sad and resentful as I imagined them anticipating the arrival of Christmas morning and the excitement of their kids as they discovered what Santa had left them. I sat on the curb outside the Prince home and stared at the Nichols home opposite, wondering just what traditions *they* had and how excited their kids would be that night.

Before long I began to cry. I felt so out of place, so desperate and misunderstood. I was so far from being the nice kid down the street that I wanted to be and felt so distant from what others expected of me. I was lost inside. I had no direction and no idea how to get it. Unsteady on my feet, I stumbled as I tried to stand up from the curb, and fell. I rolled over and looked up at the sky—snow had started to fall.

As I walked back to the house, I couldn't tell whether the dismalness inside me was coming from my emotions or from the vodka. Either way, it was the same to me. Not for the first time, I knew that I couldn't continue with this lifestyle and that I had to ask for help.

The trouble was, I just couldn't find a way to ask either the Prince or Nichols families to try to understand what I had been through and to help me get on the right track. I knew, as I had always felt I knew, that none of them could possibly imagine what the last twelve years had been like for me and why I would deliberately and desperately self-destruct. Their lives were so different, and what I had been through would be so foreign to them, that they simply wouldn't know how to help, or even if they could.

After all, *I* was *living* this life, and I didn't know what to do. How could I expect that anyone else would?

5

GOING OVER THE EDGE

Real love is very difficult to understand. For me, as a teenager, it was all but impossible to understand. It was so foreign to me; I just didn't know what it was. During those years, I managed to bury my emotions and my fears even deeper than I had done as a child. I was cold and heartless. My heart was filled with years of abuse and shame. There simply wasn't room for any more hurt.

The first time I actually attempted suicide, I'd failed. I had failed at everything I had ever done. This time it was a mistake—I didn't know what a heroin-cocaine mix could do.

ONE OF THE HARDEST issues I faced as a teenager—like most teenagers—was trying to sort out how to deal with my confused emotions and thoughts. I had no idea who I was or where I was going in life. Whatever the Nichols family could give me in love, respect, and confidence, Mom would strip away within moments of being around her. It was as if she couldn't bear that I was moving on and she was being left behind. It didn't matter what direction I was taking—just the fact that I was now moving anywhere away from Mom made the situation more unstable.

Once I reached what I thought was rock bottom, I turned to Judy Prince for help. One of the worst feelings I had was the way I felt when I shared some of my lifestyle and my thoughts with Judy. I had confided most of the experiences I'd had over the last few years and was more than ashamed at the lack of modesty I felt when talking to her about them. Judy had known that what I was doing was out of character, something self-destructive, yet she had no idea of the magnitude of it. I shared with her only a tiny portion of the drug use and the alcohol abuse I had fallen into. I certainly couldn't bring myself to admit to her that I had the morals of a street dog and was more than comfortable going from one girl to another. I was expecting that in some way she would know and it wouldn't have to be said.

What hurt me the most was the feeling of mistrust I created between my two halves: the one half of me trying to be a good clean kid, and the other half trying to be more outrageous and dangerous than anyone around me.

I buried the conflict and the damage it was causing me. I buried it all in that place that held my childhood; that place where no one talked back at me, no one lied about me or tried to hurt me—my diaries, and deep in my soul.

All the sleepless nights lying in my bed in a state of pure fear were just some of the memories I now tried to keep in check, to reserve for those tearstained pages. When I reread them and really thought about it, I had to force myself to keep control over my emotions. I knew that the more I thought about it, the more I lost my control.

And it was a battle I could never win. Every time I tried to push those memories out of my mind and into that place in my heart that was now overflowing, I was failing to keep the emotions from surfacing. The more I wrote, the more I recalled. All the memories of crying my heart out in the basement late at night, hiding from Mom in the storage space at the bottom of the basement landing, sleeping in the backyard bushes whenever Mom was even more drunk than usual and needed an outlet and wanted to beat the life out of me—all those horrible, hurtful memories always came back. I tried to convince myself that I was able to keep them in check, but I never actually could. Those memories and emotions always haunted me—in my sleep, all throughout the day, and even when I was stoned out of my mind. I was constantly having to force them away. Sometimes my thoughts came faster than my pen could keep up with.

The one memory that I could never put pen to paper about was of the china cabinet that stood in the front dining room in California. The base was merely five feet wide, and it was a foot and a half tall and separated in the middle by a small supporting piece of wood. The space I would run to and hide in was no more than twelve inches deep and a little more than a couple of feet long. Each time I tried to get the memory out of my head and onto the paper, I would calculate how little I must have been to fit in such a small space—and simply cried again.

The vision of that little boy, that little stuttering boy, hiding like a hunted animal, was too much for me to recall—even as a teen.

My journal had become my only true friend, but it had also become my worst enemy—it had become a true reflection of me.

I had the ability to hide and carefully keep almost anything from anyone. I was so good at hiding the past from everyone that it hurt. I had to remain loyal: loyal to myself, but also to my expectation that the bottom would drop out at any minute and I would be right back in the same old void.

That's what I really wanted, the bottom to fall out, to find myself in some sort of trouble with the law. Or even better, in a foster home somewhere far away from it all: far away from Mom and my family, far away from the kids at school, and far away from my past. I thought it would be a chance to start over. I was running away from everybody and everything.

I had been able to play the role of the shy one, the awkward, stumbling teenager, for so long that I became a master at it and used it whenever I felt my past coming to the surface.

I had been so successful at masking what was lurking underneath the surface that I was able to keep the secret of my childhood *and* my current lifestyle from the Nichols family and from my new friends. I simply allowed them their ignorance of my horrific past. I had outgrown the stuttering problem that haunted me for all of my childhood, but I couldn't overcome the shame that followed me around day to day. Simply being taller and heavier didn't mean that everything had changed. There was a lot more that I wanted just to go away on its own besides my stuttering, but that never did.

With all the care and concern of a true friend, Judy expressed her disappointment when I told her a little about my substance-abuse problems, but also her desire to help me. After several days of talking whenever the opportunity arose, she had voiced her conviction that I needed to understand the crucial importance of "self-worth" and the reason that I was placed on the earth. At this point I was so desperate for an answer that I would have done anything.

Before long I was talking to a couple of young Mormon missionaries, and with the help of the Prince and Nichols families, we scheduled discussions at one or the other of the families' houses. I began to understand that I wasn't alone in my struggles.

John and Darlene were supportive of my change in attitude and began to share with me their beliefs and the reasons they seemed to hold it all together. Rob and Judy, like the Nichols family, made sure that I had a place to ask questions and that I felt comfortable in asking. I now began to be able to express gratitude, and even love, to those around me. I began to be at ease when Darlene or John hugged me—I noticed that I didn't freeze and stop breathing every time they came near me. The occasional smile that leaked out of my face was genuine—frightening, but genuine.

John and Darlene gave me the confidence to speak, the comfort to express my thoughts and not be ashamed of being alive. They never once put me down or reminded me of how pitiful I looked, how bad I smelled, or how stupid I was. With the support and emotional respect they showed me, I was able to slightly loosen that stranglehold I kept on my emotions and feelings.

I had hidden all my feelings so deep and for so long that it was incredible to rediscover them.

Judy had warned me of the challenge it would be to maintain my newfound feeling of security and happiness with myself when I was at home. Constantly, she would remind me that whatever happened between Mom and me, I must bring to mind the answers to my questions about self-worth and self-pride so as to overcome the bombardment of emotional abuse Mom powered out.

Once Mom discovered that I was having discussions with Mormon missionaries, she began to degrade and bad-mouth the Mormon Church as often as she could. Within a few weeks I had learned that she had been raised Mormon and knew all about it. I was surprised to discover that she had full knowledge of the answers that I had sought for so long. She had simply let them evaporate out of her life. I couldn't understand why and yet I did understand: She was ashamed, like me, of the lifestyle she now lived—the lifestyle I now lived. The self-destruction, the lies, the disconnection from reality. Mom was a mad alcoholic; I was an angry teen on drugs. There really was little difference between us.

Once Mom heard that I was serious about the possibility of joining the Church, she confided in me and showed me the years and years of genealogy that she had completed. I was dumbfounded to make the connection and understand that what she had told me as a child was true: Many of my forefathers were among the pioneers that crossed the Great Plains looking for a new home in Salt Lake Valley. She showed me birth and marriage records dating back more than one hundred and fifty years. The Mormon Church had been there throughout our family history. Many of my relatives had organized the groups that made the long trek and had eventually settled throughout Salt Lake Valley. They were the stonecutters that carved the stones for the Salt Lake Temple, the masons that spent their lives building and believing in the teachings of the Church. When Mom showed me the marriage records she told me how I was related to this person and that person.

Like so much else in my life, it was emotionally crushing to learn that Mom had the means to help me with my quest to understand, and had blindly turned away. Her life had evolved so far distant from what she was once familiar with. I knew that alcohol was what had destroyed her ability to believe in herself and help those she loved. I knew that for a long time she had been drained of her mental faculties as well. In short, she was a different person from the person she once had been. Her mental state was deteriorating further, and her actual body was barely hanging on. Her life as an adult was filled with shame and was void of direction and purpose.

I saw that my life was headed in the same direction.

Since I had discovered that Mom was more than familiar with the wealth of knowledge that I had recently been introduced to, I had to find out from Gram just what was true and what wasn't. For the first time, I actually wanted to find out whether Mom's bad-mouthing the Mormon Church was just another game she was playing to destroy something I valued.

So I spent time in Holiday, Utah, with Gram and asked all the questions that I feared the answers to.

"What was Mom like as a kid?"

"What were her friends like?"

"Was Mom always in trouble as a kid?"

"How did you discipline her?"

"Did Mom ever go to church as a child?"

I learned that all I'd suspected was true. Mom *had* been raised Mormon and chose to erase all traces of those beliefs. I learned, too, that Gram was well aware of the abusive situation at home when we were growing up in Daly City, and she, like Dad, had felt that there was nothing she could do to stop her own daughter. Gram had developed the same need I now had: the need to find another family and another sense of belonging. And she did. She simply moved on and befriended another family north of Salt Lake, and my brothers and I simply faded out of her life, as far as Gram was concerned.

With this new knowledge came a new conflict between believing what I was now being taught about life to be the truth, and the life experiences I knew to be all too real. And an awareness of just how far apart the two were. I had an overpowering need to make a choice as to which direction I would now follow. I had the chance to socialize with kids my own age and make myself fit in, and no one need ever know about my recent past or my childhood. I had the chance to start life as a teenager.

And yet I couldn't. I wasn't about to let it all end as simply as that. I couldn't simply move on, and allow the years and years of tears and pain to have been for nothing.

I wanted revenge—I wanted Mom to pay for all the hell I was raised in. I had to find some way to make her feel the pain and the shame I knew too well.

———————

The second mistake I made as a teenager was trying to serve two masters at the same time. By not making a conscious choice between my two options I lived a lie, pretending that I understood and believed in what I was being taught while secretly continuing the drugs and booze and the ungratifying and emotionless sex. I chose to hide my destructive behavior as best as I could and continue with the steps needed to become a member of the Church of Latter-Day Saints.

I enjoyed getting high more than I enjoyed the companionship of the other teens I was getting to know. None of them took any drugs or drank; they all lived clean lives. I was living a lie when I socialized with the kids from the local youth group at the Church and at the same time still sticking with my old way of life: staying out all night drinking and getting high, then desperately trying to stay awake during a Sunday service.

This time my life was really spinning out of control. The conflict became so overpowering that I was literally facing a breakdown. I just couldn't discern who I was supposed to be at any given time, or what I was supposed to be doing.

Before long I didn't know what day of the week it was, or even how to find out. As I progressed deeper and deeper into my feelings and emotions, I was also going further and further with the self-destruction. I embedded myself in drugs and alcohol to the point that my addict friends were now afraid to be around me. The friends from high school who I used to hang out with behind the gym—the ones that once thought of me as inexperienced—were now afraid of me. They knew just how far I was willing to go. Now they talked behind my back and called *me* a "junkie loser." It was so odd having once been one of the crowd picking out those older teens and identifying *them* as junkies, and now being the one that the crowd called out to and hassled. Even those few friends that I once shared with stayed away from me.

I used to be considered green, wet behind the ears, the "newbie." Now I was the one that they called "over the top."

I was using twice as much cocaine, acid, pot, crystal methamphetamine, and crack as anyone else. I had even started to "chase the dragon"—of all the drugs I tried, heroin was the easiest to get and the cheapest.

And I was showing signs of becoming violent. My previous thoughts and fears of the bottom falling out of my life eventually came to pass. Without actually trying to, I nearly killed myself with an overdose.

After a petty and meaningless argument with Mom, I convinced myself that I had not yet reached the maximum drug dose that I could handle. I wanted more and more. I wanted to get farther and farther away from Mom, from my brothers, and from myself.

One night, I took off to the local elementary school yard. I had never tried to smoke cocaine, DXM (dextromethorphan), and heroin together before but had always heard that it was so much more intense. With no particular reason other than feeling even more exhausted by my family and my life than ever, I collected a few bags of partially used cocaine and heroin and mixed them with crushed DXM pills into one bag. I looked at the gun hidden away in the baseboard and left it where it lay. I didn't have the guts for that at the moment.

Once I arrived at the school grounds, I stuffed as much as I could into the pipe I'd taken from where I kept it under my bed. Just over two ounces was more than I needed.

I knew I was in trouble when it became difficult to breathe and I felt nauseous. My stomach hurt to the point that I vomited. My heart was racing out of control, and my head began to pound; soon after, I couldn't feel my fingers.

I remember waking in my bedroom, lying on my bed fully dressed and yet still freezing. Every bone in my upper body and legs was in pain. I had been there for well over a day. No one in the house cared—no one ever asked any questions.

I later found out that using that much cocaine when mixed with heroin was bad enough, but when DXM was added it could be lethal. I now had my answer—I didn't need the gun anymore—I knew how to do it.

After dinner one night I found myself having a particularly acrimonious argument with Mom. I was being just as verbally abusive as she was and getting angrier and angrier with myself. After a while, Scott came upstairs to see what the commotion was about. Normally, Scott would cut himself off from the arguments and slip into his own room. When he heard me yelling and screaming at Mom for everything that had ever gone wrong in my life, he stepped in. Placing himself between Mom and me, he yelled: "Get the hell out!"

By this time Scott had taken on the role of father figure in the household. Mom had rewarded and even encouraged him to take part in my "punishments." From Scott's point of view he was growing up, but I knew better—I had been right where he was now. When our brother David was still living in the house, I had been the one who often colluded with Mom to make David's life hell. It was to save my own skin. I thought she would kill me if I didn't go along with it. Only, *I* knew that what I had been doing then was wrong.

Shocked and confused, I ran out of the kitchen and down to my room, retrieved my stash of cocaine and my newest escape, "crack," plus the pistol from behind the baseboard.

I ran back upstairs. When I reached the top of the steps, I opened the glass door and ran out, slamming the door hard enough to shatter the glass and send it scattering all over the steps and front porch. I was angry, and out of control with my emotions and my whole life. I was mad, physically and mentally shattered. My body was wasting away and my mental state was terrible. I had a few bucks in my pocket, and enough cocaine and crack to kill myself. And if that didn't work, I had the gun.

I ran up the street and across the side street to the school yard—just behind the Nichols family home. I found an open doorway and knelt down inside it. As I crouched there I recalled the few times that my old friends would talk about "going over the edge." When they said that, they meant crack. Occasionally some of the teens at the school I used to attend scored not only pure cocaine but once in a while crack cocaine.

I thought vaguely about the possible effects and the unknown outcome—none of my friends actually had the guts to smoke crack. Was this perhaps my chance? I was going to get so damn high, so insanely stoned that I would finally find the guts to pull the trigger.

I stood up from the doorway and tried to think about what the drug might do to me. I recalled one of the kids at school who was hospitalized after a botched overdose and how he never was the same after that.

Back inside the doorway, where I had been kneeling earlier, I pulled the stash out of my pocket. I emptied all my pockets, and held the gun in my hand. I stopped. I didn't want to do that before I'd blasted myself into a drug-induced coma. I had it planned out. First blow my mind with the stash, and then blow my mind with the gun.

I sat in the doorway holding the gun and searched for the courage to use it. I was too afraid. Once again, I turned to the stash in my pocket for some sort of answer. But I chickened out. I knew that if the police found me with the gun and I was still alive, I would be a lot worse off.

I stepped out of the doorway, released the magazine, and emptied the round from the chamber. I carefully placed the round in the top of the magazine and tossed them separately onto the school rooftop, then retreated inside the doorway. Normally I'd use my school ID card to mix and line up the cocaine, but since I had neither a flat surface nor my ID, I simply mixed the two drugs in the palm of my hand with my finger and licked my finger clean.

The taste of the two drugs combined was much like what I would expect powdered cleanser to taste like.

I looked up into the sky and said: "Go to hell!"

Leaning back into the corner, I snorted what I could until I had to stop. Within a moment, I felt the back of my tongue burn as I had never before experienced. A second later, the back of my neck and the base of my skull went numb. I could feel the real effects when my head began to feel squeezed. It was almost as if my brain were being crushed inside my skull. My heart began to pound and my chest was heaving. I'd experienced excessive drug use before, but nothing this harsh—nothing even remotely like this.

I looked in the palm of my hand. I saw drops of blood there, from my nose. I had used a little more than half of the amount. Without hesitating, I lowered my head, lifted my hand to my nose, and took another long inhale until it was gone. The burning in my head was now pure numbness. The skin on my scalp felt like rubber, and my hair was tingling as if it were falling out.

I knew I had finally gone over the edge.

I lay back against the wall. Either it was getting dark outside, or I was losing my sight. The blood coming from my nose was now a constant flow. The reaction my body was showing me was more than what I'd expected. I had used the entire amount of crack that I'd acquired a few days before and only had a small amount of cocaine and heroin left.

I had finally done it. I'd mixed cocaine and heroin and inhaled it directly into my bloodstream. It was a mistake, but I was happy that it was finally done.

The sounds of the school yard and the neighborhood kids playing gradually faded as confusion took over. I was barely able to see or hear and I was finding it difficult to breathe. I wasn't sure what was going to happen next. Whatever, it was all the same to me at that moment. I had finally done what I had set out to do all along: end my life.

6

TEMPORARY FOSTER CARE

Every once in a while, something positive comes from something so negative in our lives. At my lowest point, I took one simple step—a step in a new direction. I had to get out of that house. I had to get away from Mom. What I realized later was that in running away from myself I had only myself to blame. At one point I thought Mom was the reason my whole life was a mess. It was all her, not me. I learned the hard way that I was wrong. Looking back, had there been one really good counselor to talk to, perhaps I would have been able to change.

As I sat in the doorway I couldn't determine if I was awake or asleep. I couldn't think clearly. I was hazy about the situation I had put myself in. Sitting back, I felt the heat rush through my body, the adrenaline flowing through my arms and legs. I looked down at my feet and realized that I couldn't feel past my lower chest. All I could feel was the heaving, my desperate attempts to breathe. It wasn't clear to me at the time, but I believe I fell in and out of consciousness. Not knowing whether it was just after dusk and I had been there for a while, or whether I had partly lost my vision, I lay with my back against the doorway and desperately wanted to sleep.

I had to get rid of the blood-soaked shirt and try to wipe my face clean. I attempted to stand, but fell back onto the cement and was unable to lift my head off the ground. I managed to remove my outer shirt and stash it behind my head as I lay there. Then, out of the corner of my eye, I saw a Sandy City police car pulling up to the steps of the school entranceway some thirty feet distant. The officer came over and started to talk to me. I have no idea what he said or how I responded. Shortly after the first car arrived a second pulled up, and the two officers talked for a moment, then came back over to me. As I fell in and out of consciousness, I tried to listen and yet had no desire to. I didn't care.

Lifting me by the arms, they carried me to the back of the cruiser. As we drove off, the officer kept asking who I was and what I was doing. When he changed the subject and began talking about the seriousness of drug abuse, it became apparent that he knew I was under the influence of something.

As I listened, I understood that I was in grave trouble and would be facing grave consequences, even as a juvenile. Before long we arrived at our destination. As the officer walked me inside and placed me in a chair, I could tell that the effects of the high were wearing off. My head began to pound.

"He won't tell me his name and I found no ID. He's going to need some attention. He cut his forehead on the cement and doesn't even know it," the officer said.

A nurse came in and looked me over. She cleaned around my forehead and face. Like the officer, she knew the cause of my situation. "He's high as can be," she said to him.

As I listened to the officer talking to the woman behind the desk, it dawned on me that I was in some sort of youth detention center. I looked around. Several adults were staring at me. The discomfort of their stares combined with the pounding in my head made me angry.

I knew that my best chance of getting out of that house of hell I lived in and out of the life I had been living was to keep my identity a secret. I was more than confident that it would be several days, if not weeks, before Mom would start to feel concerned that I'd failed to come home. Another thing I knew was that she would never call the police.

Within a few hours I was transferred to a house north of Salt Lake City. We arrived just as I was starting to regain my understanding. Inside, I was introduced to the husband and wife that ran the center. There were over a dozen kids there, mostly teenage boys and a few girls. From the short, direct orientation I was given it became clear that I was being put in a sort of halfway house.

Soon I was assigned a room and a bunk in this place with half a dozen other boys, ranging in age from thirteen to seventeen. Once I had myself settled—which didn't take long as I had nothing with me—I was called down to the office and asked to reveal my identity, so my "parents" could be notified.

It suddenly struck me that I was there to stay, at least for a while, whether I gave my name or not. It would be best if, as far as possible, I refused to cooperate, so as to ensure my removal from home. I felt as if I had control over the situation, and could manipulate the system into getting just what I wanted: permanent removal from Mom's house.

Not long afterward I started to feel the same sickness I had become accustomed to after a high wears off. I was exhausted, hungry, and nauseous. At the dining hall, I saw that I was the new kid on the block and I was among several types of teenagers. Some were there for emotional issues and a few because of unfit home situations. I could almost look at the kids and tell who was there for what reason. As I looked around the hall, I noticed that one of the girls there stood out. I couldn't determine why she would be in such a place.

I took my tray and walked over and sat down at her table.

"What's your name?" she asked.

"Richard."

I fully expected the "Why are you here?" question, but she simply went on about the conditions in the home and about the couple that ran it. She described them as helpful and accepting.

As I picked at the food on my tray she asked if I had got busted for possession.

"No, I don't think so," I replied.

As I thought about what I had just said, I realized that I really didn't know why I was there. I knew that the police found me so stoned I was in and out of consciousness, but I guessed they had no idea of the amount of drugs in my system.

"I'm not sure why I'm here," I said.

"When you don't give them your name, you usually stay until they can find out who you are."

"Sounds like you've been here before," I said.

"I'm in and out of here a few times a year."

"How old are you?" I asked.

"I'm seventeen now," she told me. "They're not sure what they can do with me since I'm less than six months away from my eighteenth birthday."

I was in a similar situation. I was sure that if they found out who I was and that I was also nearly eighteen years old, they would simply return me back home. As I contemplated my situation she broke my train of thought by asking: "What are you doing after dinner?"

"I'm not sure. What should I be doing?" I asked.

She smiled. I saw straightaway that she had a different idea than what I had anticipated. I'd fully expected to be structured into some routine and strictly limited as to what I could and couldn't do.

"Come on—let's get out of here," she said.

Without hesitation I followed her out of the hall and outside into the courtyard. It was the first time I had really seen the place since I'd arrived. We walked around the courtyard to the opposite side. On one side was the boys' dorm, she said, and on the opposite side, the girls'. Since there were far fewer girls than boys at the home, the girls didn't have to share rooms.

When we'd made it to her room, I asked: "Doesn't anyone care that we're up here alone?"

"Nope, we're pretty much on our own here," she responded. "We just have to be quiet and not get caught."

Several hours later, as we left her room together, I felt confused. I had slept with someone whom I had never even seen before. I had no idea who she was, or anything about her, I didn't even know her name—and honestly, I didn't care.

With some reservation I asked, "What's your name?"

"J—they call me J," she replied.

I waited for one of us to say something more, then said, uncomfortably, "Good night."

I walked back to the opposite side of the courtyard. Once in my bunk I realized that I had stooped to a new low.

The next few days were spent the same. It was nothing more than a meaningless routine: having breakfast, lounging around watching TV until lunch, then to J's room in the afternoon, and back to my side of the courtyard at night.

By the second week I wondered if anyone back home was ever going to inquire as to my whereabouts. Pondering the possibilities, I wondered if Mom had just assumed something had happened to me, or if she just couldn't care less and had done nothing about my disappearance.

Then as I pondered it more, I recalled how I felt when I knew David was gone, and how I believed that I was the next one in line.

No!

She wouldn't.

There's no way! I thought.

I couldn't decide what was more likely: whether she was now satisfied with another one of her kids just evaporating out of her life and was starting in on my little brother Keith, or if she'd just stopped altogether.

I knew in my heart what was the more likely of the two. I felt guilt, that I had taken the opportunity to get out but unwillingly placed my little brother in the path of her abusive madness.

Within an hour, I agreed to call home and tell Mom where I was. She was invited to a joint counseling session to determine where I would be placed. I knew that the only thing that would happen was that I would be allowed to stay at the group home until I was eighteen. Then I would be on my own. If I went home, I'd be in the same situation: looking for an answer until I was eighteen.

Mom agreed to come down for a meeting, but I knew that nothing would change between us. I understood well enough that she had no intention of changing, and neither did I. We were both set in our routines and cared little about what the other thought.

She showed up at the meeting as expected. She looked like hell. She was unbathed, her hair greasy and pinned down, and she wore the same yellow moon boots she had been wearing for years. They were the only shoes that fit her feet. Since her liver was so destroyed by now, her legs had no circulation whatsoever. Those were the only things that allowed her to walk outside. Winter or summer, she always wore those old boots.

Looking like hell, stinking of booze, and with the same attitude she had before: "I don't care what he does or where he goes. I really just don't care!"

She repeated this slurred declaration to the counselor three or four times.

Over the course of twenty minutes or so, Mom was reminded several times that I was only seventeen. I was not my own legal guardian, and she was responsible for me. After hearing that a few times, she backed down, and agreed that we both needed an "out," to get away from each other.

By the end of our session we had both agreed that I would enter a youth program tailored to my situation. When a child is on the verge of being his own legal guardian and not able to reside at home, there is but one answer: to move out and be placed under the supervision of a state or local youth program.

The only way the state would allow me to leave was if I enrolled in the program I had been told about, the Salt Lake City Youth Development Enterprises. I agreed to sign up. YDE was a local organization that helped troubled teens like me. They ran a youth group that worked in the pineapple fields of Hawaii. By the end of the day I had all the information I needed, and Mom and I were on our way back home.

The only words spoken between us were short and sweet.

"You just make damn sure you're out by Wednesday. I don't care if you go to Hawaii with that group or you're living on the curb, but you're out of my house, mister," she said coldly.

"Sure," was all I could say.

Back at the house and in my room, I looked over the information I had been given and began to look forward to getting out. Anything was better than the situation at home. I had no idea how or when I would be able to get to Hawaii and join the YDE program. At the time, I didn't care. I knew I had to get out, and fast.

The only fear I still had was leaving little Keith in that house of madness. Although I had never seen Mom really take up against Keith like she did me and David, I always had this suspicion that when I left, Keith would take on the role that I took when David left—his replacement.

I'm sorry, but I have to get out of here, I said to myself quietly.

By now, I had managed to cut myself off from my own family, my new families—the Nichols and Prince families, the ones I really cared for, the ones that had really tried to help—and the people from school that I thought were my friends.

Before I could summon the courage to face John and Darlene about the way I had gotten into the youth center in the first place, I had to decide if I was going to lay it all out for them. If I did, I would have to leave the decision up to them: If they still wanted to help me, then great. If not, I didn't actually know what I'd do. The fact was, I really had no choice at that point. I had to find the courage to face my embarrassment and own up to the reckless life I'd been leading, if I wanted them to understand the whys behind how lost I truly was.

The first place I went after I made it home was to the neighborhood near my high school and back to the kids that once looked upon me as wet behind the ears. Now I wondered just what they would say, but I had little concern. All I wanted and all I needed was a solution, even if it was tempo-rary. I wanted something that would take the bad feelings away. I wanted somewhere to go where I didn't have to think about it, or think about anything.

Within a few short minutes I found my friend Nathan and obtained what I had been looking for—acid. Once again I was comfortable with the opportunity to separate myself from Mom, Scott, and the embarrassment I would feel when I told the Nichols family the truth. It was all I could think about as I walked home. All I wanted was to get away from everybody and everything—including myself, as usual.

Back in my room on my bed, I thought again about just what I would say to John and Darlene. I had no desire or intention to share with Mom what I had become, nor did I think she would care. But I knew that John, Darlene, Rob, and Judy *would* care.

The Prince and Nichols families between them had taught me that I had to face my shortcomings, and that if I believed in God enough, I would be able to seek forgiveness and to forgive myself for all my feelings. If I kept myself clean from alcohol, drugs, and anything else that would harm my body, I would find strength and peace. I saw how it worked in their lives and that it was true, yet I could never find the courage to step up and make the commitment myself.

I inventoried my actions over the last year, and I came to this conclusion: *John and Darlene couldn't understand what my life was like in California, and they can't imagine what it is like now.*

How are they going to understand that I need help? I asked myself.

Having decided that I was unable and unwilling to find a way to talk to them, I simply reverted to my previous self-destructive thoughts.

I pulled out the acid-laced postage stamps I had in my wallet, tore one in half, placed one half on the back of my tongue and the other back in my wallet. It produced a much faster reaction than I recalled, and I was anxious to reexperience the effects, so I used the other half immediately.

I lay back on my bed and experienced a high that can only be described as absolutely terrifying. I knew who I was and where I was, yet I questioned it. I knew what I had done, and yet I questioned it. I wasn't actually sure if I was really me or if I was someone else living out a dream. The hallucinations and my reckless state of mind, combined with an oncoming paranoia, left me paralyzed. I was afraid to move, yet I believed I was moving without actually doing so. I had been clean for the few weeks I was at the center, and now I'd done it all over again.

I couldn't sit still, and yet I was afraid to do anything. I took the second stamp out of my wallet and placed the whole thing in my mouth.

Suddenly I became aware that I was once again up at Mesa Park near my house. It was well after dark and I was sitting on top of the jungle gym. I couldn't recall the walk up to the park or which path I took. I couldn't recall how long I had been there, either.

As I looked across the park and over the houses I could see the telephone wires and power lines that ran from street to street. I was flying. I carefully focused my attention on the fact that I had to weave from side to side as I flew high above the houses, so that I didn't get caught in the wires.

Farther and farther I flew, past the neighborhood and out to a large lake. I was approaching the lake headed downward, and I felt sure that I would soon crash to the ground. But lifting my body up and onward, I was able to continue flying. I quickly learned that the farther I went toward the lake, the stronger my fears and anxieties became. Below me I could see an assortment of animals devouring all the other kids who had flown out that far and crashed.

The fear became panic when I couldn't force myself to turn around. As I hovered over one spot, I began to fall closer and closer to the ground. When I landed, a pack of animals was coming toward me. I ran and desperately tried to force my body back into the air and fly back toward the park. As I ran, I forced myself to fall to the ground. But with the speed and the wind behind me, I managed to gain flight, just like an airplane taking off.

Eventually I was flying back high above the lake. Faster and faster I flew, directly back toward Mesa Park and between the wires above the houses. The fear and the rush of staying between the wires, as I flew faster and faster, kept feeding me. The confidence I gained as I passed one set of wires and then another kept me going faster and faster. Now I could close my eyes and still fly deftly in and out of the wires as I made my way back to the park. At one point, just before I reached it, I was flying so high and so fast that the wires were a flash of black lines before me. In and out I wove my way through the tangled web and came closer and closer to the park.

It took me a while to accept what my feelings were really telling me. Those feelings and emotions I had hidden deep in my heart always came to the surface whenever I was high. I began to compare what I experienced on that acid trip to my life, and I saw just how close the trip was to reality. I knew in my heart that if I continued much longer with the drugs and the alcohol, I would end up a homeless junkie. I couldn't get out of my mind that image of the animals on the ground chasing me. I compared them to the kids at school who now feared me—those kids that had once taken me into the "group"—the ones that now wanted to steer clear of me, the ones that said I was bad news.

I don't recall what happened after that—I assume that it was all part of the high. I was lying on my back on top of the jungle gym, staring into the night sky. Cold, damp, and exhausted, I was now coming to. I sat up. Dawn was streaking orange across the sky as I walked back home. Once back in my bedroom, I couldn't tell what was real and what wasn't. I couldn't tell what had been a dream and what had been reality. A small part of me felt that many of the things I recalled about the acid trip were very close to the real feelings I hid deep inside me. It frightened me.

I was able to actually distance myself, and I felt no remorse, sadness, or guilt about what I'd done. All I knew was that it was Friday night or Saturday morning. I lay down on my bed and closed my eyes.

On awakening, I made my way to the bathroom, and was sick. Cold water and a washcloth usually made me feel well enough to be seen. I walked upstairs and looked through the screen door window at the newspaper on the porch. It was *Sunday* morning. I had no idea if Mom knew what I had done, or if she simply hadn't noticed that I'd slept over a day and a half.

I made my way to the kitchen, and stood there watching her as she stared at the small TV on the counter. Not saying a word, I simply retrieved a cola from the fridge and went back to my room.

I better get cleaned up before I see the Nichols family, I thought.

Once out of the shower, I saw how awful my face looked and how swollen my eyes were. My skin was off-color, and overall I looked like hell. I stared into the mirror for a few minutes. I knew that I needed help, and fast. Physically, I couldn't go on like this much longer. I would eventually kill myself if I continued. I was dressed and out the front door before anyone even noticed I was gone.

I knew the Nichols family would return from church shortly after noon and would be home if I were to call on them. But as I walked up the street I also knew I couldn't face them. I couldn't let them know what I had been through in the last few weeks. I was sure they would ask where I had been and I would make up some excuse for not being around.

Overwhelmed with shame, I turned around, walked back to the house, and went back to bed. I just couldn't face them, not now.

7

HAWAII OR BUST

I needed the support of those few who loved me and to have the right people around me if I was going to make it. John, Darlene, and Judy helped me get a grip on myself and helped me take a chance. I discovered that I'd had no idea of the damage I was capable of. I had no idea of anything. I needed to tell someone about what I was going through. I had to get it off my chest and out in the open. But I just couldn't open my mouth to anyone who knew me. It had to be someone else. It had to be someone new—someone I didn't know and who didn't know me.

I T TOOK ME A few days, but I finally found the courage to say something—not much, but just enough for them to realize I needed help.

John and Darlene had more faith in me than I had in myself. For the first time, I was able to share with them a small portion of what I had suffered as a child and what I was suffering as a teenager. I didn't share much, just the fights with Mom and a "small problem with drug abuse."

I was overcome by their support and respect. I truly felt that they loved me. In spite of all my deception and all my secrets, they showed me love and concern. They didn't condone what I had done. I shared only a portion of it. I thought that if I told even half of the real story, they might have left me behind.

"You have to get off the fence and decide. The writing is on the wall, Richard," Darlene told me.

I had never had John and Darlene become frank and assertive with me before—they had always been supportive, but they'd known next to nothing about my past. Now, with the little I'd told them, I had disappointed them as if they were my parents. I desperately wanted to be accepted and loved. I was ashamed of my actions. The big fear I had was that I lacked the courage to stop. In fact, I knew I couldn't handle going straight—not alone. I was still faced with the dilemma that had hounded me for a few years now: I didn't know what to do or who to ask for help.

I had to either let someone answer my cries for help, or stop crying for help. I had to do one or the other; Darlene was right.

I decided to revisit the recommendation of the temporary foster caregivers and determine if the YDE program of Salt Lake City was my answer.

I called the local office for the details of joining the program. YDE would interview and accept into the program certain kids under the age of eighteen who either couldn't or wouldn't live at home anymore. Kids who needed the support of adults without the stigma associated with other "programs." I set up an interview and got the answers to all my questions. It took less than ten minutes for them to decide if I could be a candidate. I learned what was available and what I had to do before the deadline to enroll.

YDE operated two programs based in Hawaii, and provided the opportunity for young people to get jobs and learn the basic skills of being on their own. By the end of the week I had decided that I was getting into one of those programs if it killed me—before I killed myself.

I knew that I needed to not only get away from the house but out of Sandy City, Utah. If I stayed there much longer my self-destructiveness would plumb new depths. I was afraid of myself and of what I might do. There was no fear of embarrassment left in me, or of the consequences, the costs, or the effects of my overindulgence in drugs, booze, sex, or anything else.

I made the arrangements and was ready to leave for Hawaii. Gram had bought me a fifteen-dollar metal chest at Kmart and a few clothes. The day I left, when I told Mom I was leaving, I felt that it was the beginning of the end for her and me. I was now on my way to my new life. The cost of the trip out was not difficult to manage. I had no car, no social life, and no real expenses, other than the habits that shadowed my life. Gram had convinced Mom that the four hundred dollars I was short for the cost was worth the investment to get me out of the house. I have no idea how she arranged it or how she paid it, but she did.

Gram was waiting outside. She had said she would drive me to the airport and make sure I got on the plane. I think she knew that I wasn't trustworthy and wanted to make sure I really got to Hawaii.

"I'm going to the airport now," I said, standing by the front door. I waited for a response. Anxiously, I waited, but Mom said nothing. I closed the door behind me.

"So be it!" I said.

I'm sorry, Keith, but if I don't get out now, I never will. God help you, because I can't, I thought, as I walked away.

In an odd way, I felt sorry for her. I had told her that I was going to find a way to get out, and I had. Now that it was a reality, she simply didn't acknowledge me. It was as if I were already gone, already out of her life.

The ride to the airport was quiet. As we drove I couldn't get Keith off my mind. I felt so bad that he was being left behind. I wondered if David ever felt that way about me when he was rescued.

The more I thought about Mom's simple, emotionless reaction to my leaving her, the more I understood that I was dead to her, just like "It" was when he left. There was no need to speak to me—to her, I didn't exist anymore.

I thought about the lives that had dissolved in Mom's corrosive presence, the lives that she had changed forever. My father, who simply stopped coming home one day; my oldest brother Ross, who ran as far as he could the first chance he got; David and what he went through; and now me. I so desperately wished I could take Keith with me. But I couldn't. I had to leave him behind. I couldn't understand myself, I couldn't take care of myself, so how could I help my younger brother, whom I loved?

I spent the five-hour flight to Hawaii thinking about Keith and what I feared he would now endure: a life of pain, shame, and fear that most people couldn't imagine. During the flight, in between my worries about leaving Keith behind and the thoughts of a new life, I desperately tried to sleep. It was no use.

My destination was the island of Lanai. By the end of the day, and several thousand miles away, the plane had landed.

On Lanai, I was placed with a stranger, another kid from Salt Lake named Kyle. The house I found myself in had two dorms, each dorm had six rooms, and each room had two teenagers. There were eight or so dorms in the place altogether, and all had the same kind of kids from all over the country—from Michigan, California, Utah, and Idaho—all with their own issues and their own reasons for being there. Like I had at the foster home, I could look at the kids and determine who had emotional issues and who had personal issues. Before long I befriended a couple of them and we started to share a little about the reasons why we were there.

In each of the dorms lived a group leader we called Luna. They were adults trained to deal with troubled kids, and from the first day they seemed to focus on a few kids in particular. These were the ones who were either shy or holding back from the group atmosphere that was created by all of us sharing in the household duties and working together.

As I expected, my turn soon came to talk to the group leaders and go through an analysis of my issues and my shortcomings. I wasn't very comfortable with talking to Luna Craig, our group leader. He wasn't very receptive to the feelings I was relating. When I mentioned the very few events that I felt I could share about my past, he told me that I had more issues than even I realized.

"I don't know why you think you have to make up such outrageous stories to get accepted here, Richard. There is no reason to make your mother out to be some kind of lunatic," Craig said.

I couldn't believe it—I had finally found the courage and the setting to open up, even if only a little. Sitting in front of me now was the first man in the world to whom I had ever confided what Mom was like, and he didn't believe me. I'd told him about one of the times I ran away and ended up in an ambulance and then the hospital, *and he didn't believe me.*

I needed to find out whether or not *I* was the one who was crazy.

For as long as I could remember, I'd always wondered if *I* was the one that was "over the rainbow," "had toys in the attic," "bars on the windows." From my earliest memories I always believed that I *was.* As a young child, I just couldn't understand how someone you loved could turn on you in a heated rage and hurt you so badly that at times you just wanted to die—and then instantly turn back into "Mommy." I knew of no other kids that ever went through one tenth of what I had been through except my older brother, but he was gone. It had to be me that was the deranged one. That must have been why I wanted to self-destruct. It was me the whole time, not Mom. I was the one who caused her to become outraged. I knew that she didn't treat the other boys like that, so it *had* to be me.

Yet I knew what I was telling Craig was true.

Our conversation was cut short when I refused to talk anymore about my history. I knew that the more I said the more I would be branded a liar and a troubled kid. Our conversation ended with Craig saying: "I think you need to speak to Clay."

Clay was one of the camp senior leaders. He was a gentle, kind man; he was able to listen and talk *with* me—not *at* me. But it wasn't long before I got a similar response from him. It was just too outrageous that a mother could actually do those things to her own kids.

As I fully expected, I was labeled "a storyteller," and it was clear that I needed "special attention." Word was spreading throughout the camp. I was furious that Clay, one of the few people I'd started to open up to, would even think about breaking my confidence.

———————

I was asked to attend a counseling session after working the pineapple fields and to speak with different leaders in the group to try and find out why I was so angry with my mom. I discovered that several of the camp leaders had written to her asking for some background information, to try to get some notion of what it was that made me so angry. The weeks went by, and I was told that Mom had not yet responded, but I was not to take it personally.

I knew that she considered me out of her life for good, and that she would never respond. And she had good reason not to speak to any of the leaders or the counselors.

As the months went on, I found that here on Lanai, Hawaii, I was the same person I had been in Daly City, California, and in Sandy City, Utah. I had the same confused feelings and the same anger that I had known for years now. My hopes that a new setting might change my outlook faded just as fast as my hopes that the counselors would help me. I was the same teenager, in a new part of the world. I had accomplished nothing by leaving home. No one in Daly City would have believed me, no one in Salt Lake believed me, and now no one in Hawaii believed me, either. The main thing I learned from my counseling sessions was that no matter where I was, I was still me, and no one would ever believe what I had to tell them or help me understand any of it.

By now I was back to my old ways and starting to make friends with the kids that I thought would have experience of drugs and alcohol.

Each week we were allowed to take a specified amount out of our checks and spend it as we desired. Some of the kids would spend it on movies and some would spend it on junk food. I finally found kids who had connections with some of the most outrageous drugs I had ever known: hash-and-opium-laced Thai sticks.

After work and after we had settled in one Friday night, two of the kids from another dorm and I snuck out and walked the short distance up to the top of one of the nearby hills. Not far from the dorms was a patch of bamboo growing wild, untouched and completely natural. The smell was incredible, and the eerie feeling as we walked through the little forest added to the heady atmosphere and to our intoxication.

We had managed to pool our money and purchase several Thai sticks. I had used hash before, but it was nothing like what I experienced in that bamboo forest. One of the kids had brought with him a bottle of vodka that he had swiped from the local liquor store the night before. On the way up to the bamboos we passed the bottle from one to another.

By the time we had made it to the middle of the forest, we had finished the bottle. For a while we sat around talking about the others in the group. Then one of the kids pulled out a Thai stick and passed it around. I was told that it was made of hashish from Thailand and laced with opium. I quickly realized what made it so special. As I stared through the forest into the light beyond, I had no idea who or where I was. I couldn't tell if what I thought was happening around me was reality or not.

I was soon out of my mind with paranoia, and the other two kids were, too. We were all so high that at first we couldn't even find our way out of this patch of bamboo that we had been to a hundred times before. It was several hours later that we finally made it back to our dorms. A few of the other kids noticed me as I stumbled in. They assumed I was either drunk or high.

All I remember from that episode is the early morning hours, when a few of the other teenagers thought it would be funny to play games with me. From time to time one of them would open the door to my room and make some funny comment, then close the door quickly. I laughed and laughed. It wasn't really funny; it was just the effect of the drugs, combined with what I thought was happening around me. Again, I couldn't tell if it was real or if it was part of the high.

By the time morning arrived word had gotten back to the counselors about what had been happening during the night. I woke, hungover and hungrier than I'd been since I arrived. Usually I made it to the mess hall before nine in the morning, but today I got there just before they closed the doors, at eleven.

As I walked the quarter mile to the hall, I met up with one of the kids I had been out with the night before. We walked along the road together, reminiscing about our night out. We laughed at each other's stories of what had happened when we returned to our dorms.

Just outside the doors to the mess hall stood Clay, the senior counselor.

"I want to see you in my office now," he barked at me.

My friend and I looked at each other.

"I've got to eat something first. I'll be up in a while," I said.

The two of them walked back to the camp, and I sat down to my breakfast. When I'd finished, I went outside and sat on one of the benches in the courtyard just outside the mess hall. I knew that the counselors would probably send me packing, as they had with other kids who broke the rules. Without reservation or remorse I walked back to camp and up to the offices, to find Clay. I didn't care. I didn't care if I was sent home.

What would be so different? I thought.

Dale, another group counselor, was in the office. He had a reputation for being the camp's hard-nosed disciplinarian. He informed me that he'd called my mom back on the mainland and told her that I was being expelled, and that she'd have to pick me up at Salt Lake City airport.

"The problem we have here, Richard, is that your mom doesn't give a damn what happens to you. She told me that you're not welcome in Salt Lake—ever. Since you're not eighteen and we're not your legal guardians we can't send you back without permission.

"What's wrong with your mother? She said she didn't care if you died and were buried in Hawaii."

I simply looked at him. "You're the ones who thought I was out of my mind. You're the ones that thought I was making up what she was really like. Now you're asking *me*?

"I don't care if you send me back home. You can drop me off at the airport and I'll take care of myself. Either one, Salt Lake International or San Francisco, it doesn't matter to me," I yelled.

The look on his face was nothing less than total bewilderment. He was shocked to think that he had me under his control one moment, then a moment later was powerless to discipline me the way he was used to doing with all the other kids who messed up. He asked me to sit where I was and wait for him to return.

In a moment he came back with Clay, and closed the door.

"I spoke to your mom and she really doesn't care what happens to you. She won't give us permission to send you back alone. She won't pick you up and she doesn't want you back in Salt Lake," Clay calmly told me.

The first chance I had to get a word in, I blurted out: "I don't care what you want to do. I'm not going back to Salt Lake. I'm getting off in San Francisco and staying there. Since you're not my legal guardian you can't stop me."

Clay asked Dale to step out of the room, then closed the door. He said softly: "Listen. I was wrong when I didn't believe you during our talks. I didn't believe you when you said that she was completely uninterested in you and your brothers' lives. I just can't understand how she can completely write you off as if you were dead."

"Let me guess. She said, 'I don't care if that son of a bitch comes back in a pine box.' She's told me that a thousand times before," I said.

The look on Clay's face was beyond shock. He was dumbfounded. Silence filled the room as we stared at each other.

"I'll make you a deal," he said. "We'll make some changes and we'll both start over fresh. But I'm telling you, any more alcohol or drugs and I'll find a way to get you out of here. Deal?"

"Deal!" I agreed.

By the time I left the office, I felt I had finally got some-where—reached someone that I could talk to and that would try to understand. I could tell Clay was really interested in helping me understand who I was and what I was doing to myself.

Within the next week I was to move to the island of Maui with a whole new group of kids, and Clay. I was told that they had to move me and tell the other kids that I'd been sent home, or they wouldn't have any control over them. It was okay with me. Soon I was on a small plane to my new home just a few miles away. It seemed like another world, another chance.

8

A Second Chance

Finally I came to the conclusion that I was the one that had to get my life in order—not God. It wasn't God that needed another chance from me; I needed to give myself another chance. I had to find the courage and the strength to forgive myself and allow myself another chance to grow up.

THE NEW SURROUNDINGS WERE almost what I had expected. The plantation house was larger than the dorms on Lanai. Maui was a much larger island. Having Clay there made it easier for me to fit in. The first day, I was asked to meet him at the main house, where he introduced me to the other counselors and the other teens. Clay and I, in a private talk earlier, had agreed that we had made mistakes on Lanai and we should both try to understand each other a little better and work toward a common goal.

"What I need you to do is to find out what you want to accomplish here on Maui and how the two of us can work toward it," he told me.

Now I had another chance to seek help, to try to understand why I was comfortable with being so self-destructive. I now had someone who wasn't *too* close to me, yet was close enough to see and understand what I was going through. I felt comfortable with Clay and his desire to understand and help me.

I left the main house to walk back to my room. I strolled out into the fields behind the house and through the pineapples, then down the red clay road. I would probably never again have a chance like I had now, I decided. I knew that Clay would be able to help me get past the issues I had. I knew that I could confide in him, and had confidence that I would be able to leave when I was ready and never see him again. It had never before struck me so forcibly that what I'd needed all along was the security of talking to someone that wasn't too close to the situation. That way I wouldn't feel as though I was being judged. John and Darlene were too close, I felt too much emotion for them. I was so afraid of disappointing them that I seldom shared much more than a few minor problems. Finally I had the desire to open up and see if I really was as crazy as I'd always thought I must be.

I walked about a mile into the fields, and found myself completely alone. One of the many times I've acted on the need to talk to God was at that moment. I knelt down in the clay at the side of the road.

I'm sorry. I didn't get the message the first time.

If you help me understand I will quit the drugs.

If you help me learn who and what I am or why I'm here, I'll listen.

Please?

As I awaited a response, a feeling of comfort came over me. I recalled the previous times that I felt this kind of emotion. I thought back to when I was much younger, holding a gun in my hand, and the voice that had scared me into backing down, making me lower the gun and walk away from Mom's bedside. I recalled the time I begged God to take my life the night before I met Darlene Nichols. The same emotion came over me now. A voice seemed to tell me that I was going to be okay. In my privacy and my solitude, among the fields that stretched for miles, I began to cry.

With a feeling of great relief, I cried. I cried for the fear of not knowing if I could do it. I cried with gratitude that God had finally heard me. I cried about all the time I had wasted. I cried because it had taken me so long. Most of all, I cried because I simply hadn't cried in years. I had vowed to myself never to let anyone see me cry for any reason, ever again.

After a while I regained my composure and lay back on the soft red clay. I looked at the sky. Either I hadn't noticed before, or I had refused to see, the incredible clearness and deep blue of the sky, the warmth of the breeze, and the smell of the salt air from the ocean that surrounded the islands. I had been in Hawaii, one of the most beautiful places on earth, for over six months, and I was only now appreciating its beauty. I was so comfortable in my spot by the side of the road that I stayed right there, and before long I faded off to sleep.

I awoke to the softness of the rain as the fresh drops fell on my face. Even the rain seemed warm and inviting. I wondered as I stood up and started to walk back to the dorms, just what else in life I had allowed myself to miss. What else had I refused to see as I had gone about my selfish and destructive lifestyle?

I'm three thousand miles away in Hawaii!

I've finally found someone I can talk to.

"I want to go straight!" I said aloud.

For the first time I truly felt like I wanted to live a morally clean and drug-free life. As I walked I pondered, taking an inventory of what I had been through. Then I recalled all those times I spent crying and wiping the tears off the pages as I wrote in my journal as a small child. I wondered where those old journals were now. I vowed to start again and capture on paper all that I had been through.

At the age of eighteen I'd been living a lifestyle I once feared. Back in middle school and early high school I had feared the kids who used drugs. Looking back I knew that I had not only passed that point, but I had become the one that even "stoners" would walk away from. I was finally ready to put a stop to my childish and irresponsible ways.

By the time I made it back to the dorms, the rain had stopped and I was happy with myself. In the courtyard, I saw that the ground was dry: the rain hadn't reached the house. Perhaps the rain was an acknowledgment from God, perhaps it was his way of washing away my past and giving me a chance to start anew.

Over the next several weeks, Clay and I spent just the right amount of time together. We always did so in certain settings, so that the other teenagers had no notion of how much he was counseling me. We would take walks around the compound, or sit at the back of the atrium during a movie and talk quietly. Over time, Clay and I were able to tell when either of us was becoming insensitive to the other's feelings—we could read each other's face.

By May 1982 I had been clean for a month and felt better than I had in years. I was able to sleep at night with my eyes closed—most of the time—and wake with a sense of purpose. All the time I spent as a child training myself to sleep with my eyes open was very necessary at the time. But now I found that I had to remember the fact that Mom was nowhere around me and that I was not in danger anymore. My health improved and I no longer looked like death. I had regained the weight I had lost over the last few months.

I felt like I was becoming me. I was more than comfortable with myself, and I was feeling pretty good about life. I was working on the issues that Clay suggested for me, and I was making progress with finding the answers to the whys that had eluded me for so long.

Everything was going smoothly until Saturday, June 5, 1982, when I received a letter from Mom. She had apparently heard from Clay, asking her to take a few minutes to think about reconciling her feelings toward me, in the hope that we would be able to rebuild a halfway normal relationship.

I usually received no mail, and was excited to get something from Sandy City, Utah. I opened the letter, and was shocked to read what she had written.

In a few short sentences she reiterated what I had known all along. She had no intention of seeing me come back to Salt Lake. As far as she was concerned, she said, I was dead. What really upset me was what came at the end of her letter: She was able to get on with her life, she informed me, now that she had finally got rid of the last thing in her life she regretted after Dad and David—me.

She acknowledged she had "issues," but brushed it off as due to the great strain of being a single parent. She went as far as to say that she accepted she was an abusive parent, but since it was only me and "that other one" (David), it was okay. She now intended to focus on Keith and make sure that he had the things in life that David and I had never had.

Her closing words suggested she was being sincere. But I didn't really know if I could believe her or not. I had no way of knowing.

She closed with a simple: "Go to hell—don't come back to Salt Lake."

I kept the letter to myself for a while. Over the next few days Clay and I talked about how I was feeling. He asked if I had received anything from Salt Lake yet.

"I did receive a letter from Mom, but it was nothing I really want to talk about. Why?" I said.

"I asked your mother to take a few minutes to send you a small present for your birthday. I didn't want the chance to pass by for her to let you know she loved you. What did she send you?"

I handed him the letter I'd kept in my pocket. As he read it, I could tell where he'd got to by his facial expressions. Once he got to the end he simply handed it back to me and said: "I'm sorry. I had no idea that she could do that."

"I did. I'm not really worried about it, I just deal with it," I snapped.

We talked about the letter from Salt Lake, about how I was doing and where I was in my struggles. As we talked, I faded in and out of listening to Clay. Mom's letter was pre-occupying me. I just couldn't get it out of my mind. Then the way Clay reacted, as if he was shocked to read her words. Hadn't he learned *anything*?

Within a few minutes I started to feel that same feeling I got whenever I wanted to just get away from it all and get as high as humanly possible—and beyond.

When our conversation was over, I took a stroll out to the pineapple fields. For over two hours I struggled with the urge to go off the deep end again, while at the same time wanting to show not only myself, but Clay, too, that I could master this continuing relationship with Mom. I knew in my heart that she was simply a drunk, and a mean one at that. I knew she had no self-respect and enjoyed dragging others down to her level to make herself look better, and I wanted no part of that.

I had to find a way to get over her either constantly being on my mind or the reason I went off on some tangent. I had to find a way to just let her go, fade away. All along I'd wanted to rebuild whatever was salvageable and take another shot at making something of our relationship; but I also wanted just to end it altogether and walk away for good. I knew in my heart that somehow I loved her as a mother— but I wouldn't give her the time of day. I had vowed to myself that, if it ever came to it, I would make sure she wasn't homeless, but I wouldn't do much beyond that. In some overriding way I loved her; and I hated her for it.

As I walked, I pondered the fact that these two feelings had been bothering me down the years: on the one hand, loving someone who was evil and completely devoid of any conscience, while at the same time hating her. Perhaps the issue that I had been fighting all this time was really with me and not her.

For the next several weeks I put more effort into staying clean than I had ever done before. I was able to control the desires and the feelings of failure, once I understood what caused those feelings. It had been nothing more than a lack of understanding, and a lack of desire to understand. I had been planning on the possibility of failure in my new attempt so that I wouldn't be overly disappointed. I knew I wasn't going to be able to stay in Hawaii forever. I was finishing the last few weeks of the season and looking forward to taking some time off. Before I left I was able to take a couple of weeks to tour the main island and a few others. The places I saw were so beautiful; I was sure I would never have the chance to see them again.

The two weeks passed and I had prepared myself for one last confrontation with Mom. I was now ready. And it had all been made possible by one man who cared enough to provide me with one more chance to learn what I should have learned ten years before. Clay gave me more than a second chance, he gave me hope.

9

"I'm Sorry"

I couldn't believe it. She'd cheated me yet again. Mom was off the hook, and I was left with the memories that she had lost somewhere along the way. I was mad, I was furious, I was explosively angry. And yet, I felt sorry for her.

WHILE I WAS IN Hawaii I was supposed to keep up with my high school program and complete several tests and other requirements in order to receive credit as a student abroad. Of course I put as little effort into it as possible, but I managed to make the grades and become eligible to graduate from high school. I knew that when I applied myself, I could not only make the grades, but good ones. It was actually quite easy. I had known that I could slack off for a really long time, then in one step catch up and deliver very high marks—when I wanted to. I knew my graduation from high school was important. I had to return to my high school in Salt Lake and finish the last classes before graduation. That also meant I had to stay with Mom while I floated through my last few weeks of school.

In Salt Lake I found Mom to be different. She looked years older—her hair and her face wore more years than her age told. Something was wrong with her. I had no idea at the time, but she was well on her way to drinking herself to death.

We didn't talk much about anything I'd done or what I'd seen in one of the most beautiful places on the planet. She couldn't care less. Disappointed yet satisfied with her low-level reaction to me being back in her house, I simply faded into obscurity once again as I finished the last few weeks of high school before graduating.

I was okay with her being short with me and demonizing me; I was okay with her ignoring me whenever it came to "her family." But I became more and more annoyed with her bringing up the past. I could understand her feelings about me during the last couple of years. Things I had done recently still made her mad. But she insisted on bringing up things that I used to do wrong as a child. She was still drinking as much as a gallon of straight vodka per day: that hadn't changed.

One of the easiest ways I found of getting out of any situation with Mom was work. I'd been working at the 7-Eleven convenience store down the street on 13th East in Sandy City for a few weeks now. I had gotten the job right after I came back from Hawaii and needed money for a car. Mom had always refused to sign for my driver's license as a minor, so I'd had to wait until I was eighteen to get it on my own.

Anytime after work, if I came back and found Mom to be in one of her drunken stupors, I would walk out and go back to work. It was never hard to pick up another shift and make a few more bucks. After a few weeks of this Mom realized that I was completely avoiding her, and it made her mad. Also, my older brother Scott was complaining that I was never there to help out with any chores.

Finally Scott had had enough. He convinced Mom that the garage needed to be cleaned out again. We started early one Saturday, and worked the entire day on cleaning out old boxes that hadn't been opened since we'd moved there from Daly City several years before. It was well after dark when Scott decided that the garage was now acceptable to him. Mom and I stayed and finished up the sweeping and did a final tidy-up, moving back in anything we'd taken outside.

We started to talk. It had been years since she and I just talked about something other than how much we hated each other. It was time for a break, anyway. She wanted a drink and I took her up on her offer of a beer. In the space of an hour we talked about the house, about the way Mom enjoyed being out of California—about almost anything that didn't matter to either of us. She seemed comfortable with me, and I was comfortable with her. Mom had a few more drinks and I had a couple more beers. That was my mistake . . .

We were back in the garage reminiscing about the boxes we had discovered while cleaning up, and recalling better times—almost foreign territory to me. She was relaying stories of all the kids being together and playing at the Russian River back in California. I had vague memories of the river, nothing much. Having fun as a family wasn't one of them.

As we discovered new boxes, we would quiz each other about what we remembered about certain events. I discovered that Mom really didn't remember a lot about being abusive when we were kids. She had no recollection at all of being the vicious drunk. As I pried more into what she did remember, it became clear that she truly had no idea of half of the things she had done in the last fifteen years.

We brought out a few more beers and she fetched the bottle of vodka out to the garage as we went through yet more boxes.

"Do you remember when the neighbors' house was shot at in Daly City?" I asked.

"No," she said.

"How about the time my bike was stolen when I was really little?"

"No, I don't recall that, either."

"Do you remember the first time I rode in an ambulance?" I asked her.

"You rode in an ambulance? Why?" she asked.

I couldn't believe it. She actually had no idea what she had done.

I was furious with her, and yet felt sad that she had slipped away like this. The woman I had known was gone. I couldn't decide if I was angrier at her losing the memories *I* had and that she should have lived with for the rest of her life, or angrier over the unbelievably simple way she'd got out of any guilt or remorse.

Looking at the pile we had created in the middle of the garage, I recalled the way I kept my room as a child. How I would pile up furniture and other belongings in the middle, just to be able to keep Mom at arm's length when she was drunk and looking for a fight.

"Do you remember the furniture in my room?" I asked her.

"I know you kept a lot of junk and it was always in the way—"

"Do you know why I did that?" I interrupted her.

"No. I guess I never asked," she said.

The more we talked, the angrier I was getting. The few beers I'd had just added to my rage. I was furious at the fact that she was able to simply brush off the way she'd treated me over the last fifteen years, yet at the same time saddened that she truly had no idea of who she was back then, and couldn't even remember any significant details about her own kids.

I pressed on: "What about David? What happened between you and David?"

"I'm not sure, I know I wasn't the best mom, but I really don't know why he was the way he was . . . Richard, I know I had issues back then, but you had problems, too. You weren't the best son, you know."

"No, I guess I wasn't," I said to her, sincerely enough.

Looking back at me as we edged around the far side of the pile, Mom stumbled over the ladder that was leaning against the wall. She fell on her side against the concrete. Instantly I felt concerned for her and rushed over to help her up. Her head was cut and she was bleeding just above the eye. I reached out my hand to her and, as if in slow motion, she hesitated, and I did too. I felt some difficulty reaching out to help her, and I'm sure she felt something similar at accepting it. But she took my hand, and I helped her upstairs and into the bathroom. As I reached for her hand, I recalled the time I was lying on the couch in the front room in California when my eye was bleeding from one of her "lessons."

The cut was fairly deep and required stitches. But she was adamant about not going to the doctor and for me to just do the best I could with a Band-Aid and towels. As I washed the wound I saw how deep it was, and the fact that she was now physically hurt upset me. But she showed no emotion about the wound. She was only concerned about me making sure she wouldn't have to get help from anyone else.

I realized that between the extra vodka and the constant state of intoxication she normally was in she really did feel no pain. As I saw to the wound I felt sorrowful when I looked in her eyes. I recalled her wedding picture where she was one of the most beautiful women I had seen. She seemed at the time to carry herself with pride. Now, as I looked at her, I saw the scars from the years and years of hatred and alcohol. I felt both pity and a sense of shame: pity for her loss, and shame for her current state.

The minutes passed, and neither of us said a word as I cleaned up the cut as best I could.

She shocked me when she broke the silence: "I want you to know how hard it has been for me. I know I can't remember a lot of what happened before, and I feel sad about that, but I just can't go back there. I just can't. It hurts too much."

"*It hurts too much?*" I snapped back, infuriated that she should assume she was the only one hurt. To say I was shattered would be nearer the mark. I just couldn't believe that she knew she had permanently damaged the lives of several of her children and yet couldn't recall the details.

Here I was, helping her and feeling pity for her, and yet she was coming out of it innocent, almost, by reason of insanity.

I felt robbed. I felt like she had the final victory over me. She had a "Get Out of Jail Free" card and didn't even know it.

"Why do you hate me now?" I asked her. "You really don't even know me."

"I don't hate you—I guess I'm . . . jealous," she said.

"*What!!!*"

"You have friends, you have freedom—you have love."

"What do you mean, I have love?" I retorted.

"The Nichols family—they've taken you in and helped you when I couldn't, and they loved you when I wouldn't." As she spoke, she took my head between her hands and turned it toward hers.

I was speechless.

I couldn't tell if I wanted to hug her or slug her.

"I'm sorry, Richard. I'm sorry for what I've put you through. I'm sorry for the time I lost with you."

"What about David?" I asked.

"I really don't remember much. I just can't find where all that has been buried," she said softly.

She knew that over time she had forced herself to erase the pain and the shame. She was now living on what she was being told, and had the luxury of not knowing if it was true or not.

Inside I was crushed—crushed for her. I wanted to say: "I forgive you," but the words never came.

At that moment she was stronger than I had ever been. In her way, she was facing her life and simply accepting who she was. I had struggled with that all my life, and now I was helping the very one that I had loathed for so long. I was ashamed of myself.

All I could say to her was: "I'm sorry. I'm so sorry."

She went directly to bed.

"Good night, Mom," I said as I walked out of her room.

I hadn't said that to her in at least twelve years. I went downstairs to my room and sat on the edge of the bed. I was so confused with the way I felt about her, and it bothered me more than I was willing to admit. It just ate at me that she was able to get herself off the hook so easily and walk away from it all, while I spent every waking minute trying to understand.

Taking my windbreaker, I left the house. I was on my way to Mesa Park when I realized that I needed to be somewhere else. Somewhere I wouldn't be troubled by the memories of years past when I would hang out after getting high as a kite.

I smoked myself into the Stone Age there, I thought.

I passed the park and walked to the top of the street. I could hear the sounds of people playing basketball in one of the church buildings there. Through the open gym doors I saw several teenage kids playing. I slipped inside and sat on the sidelines watching, unnoticed. I couldn't help but feel that I should be that carefree and comfortable with myself. I was jealous of their freedom. I knew that the freedom I was jealous of was the freedom from the ever-present consciousness of *self.*

Before I could be noticed I got up and walked out. I found my way back home and went to bed. Overwhelmed with a sense of loss, I lay there and cried. All my life and all my struggles seemed for nothing. The very reason, the very cause, of my issues was Mom, and now she was free of it all. I'd carried that around like a rock, too heavy to lift, for so long.

I awoke. I was going to be late for school. I hurried to get out of the house and on my way. But once there, I found that all I could think about was Mom and her state of mind. She had little real memory left. She was truly schizophrenic. I knew that her health was on a rapid downhill slide and that she was probably close to losing her mind altogether.

By fourth period, I had found several of the same friends I had hung out with before I went to Hawaii. I had been avoiding them since I got back, to give myself a chance to stay clean. It took all of four seconds for me to agree to go out past the football field and hop the fence, to a party at one of the kids' houses.

I stayed there for most of the school day and once again found the temptations of alcohol and cocaine too much to pass up. Given my current emotional state, my confusion over Mom, and the hundred dollars burning a hole in my pocket, there was no reason not to.

By the end of the afternoon I was unable to walk back to school, home, or anywhere else. I was trashed—I couldn't put two words together. I'd spent the hundred dollars on cocaine, and then some. I owed the kid at the house more than two hundred on top of the original hundred.

Here I was, right back where I'd been so many times before: afraid, ashamed, and embarrassed over my actions—and not giving a damn.

I convinced myself that I deserved some time away from *me*. For so many years I'd had little incentive to look any deeper than the surface of things. Before Hawaii, I didn't dare really try to understand myself, or the reasons I did what I did—it was just too much to take in. Now, seeing what Mom had finally done—that she'd convinced herself she couldn't recall anything because it was just too painful—I'd slipped back again. It was so much easier to ignore it, to simply forget it. In a way, I was just like her. We had both failed to understand that what we had done to each other we had also done to ourselves.

We'd completely disregarded our self-pride, our self-esteem, and our real reasons for going out of control. Neither of us cared about each other or about ourselves.

I guess I'm sorrier than I thought, I said to myself as I left the house that I'd spent the afternoon in and walked back toward Mulberry Way—back home.

10

BUSTED

I was back where I'd been for most of my life. I had lied to myself for years. I was out of control again. I had lied to my friends about being morally clean and drug-free. Everything I had been doing was a lie—I was living a lie—I was afraid of myself. I just couldn't face reality. And I had no idea that I could go as far as I did. Looking back, I can't believe I was stupid enough to go back to it. I was out of my mind.

I had a reputation for causing severe and permanent damage to myself and everyone around me.

It was the most outrageous, the most powerful drug I knew of.

It was heroin.

It was perfect.

I WENT STRAIGHT TO BED. It was just after dark and I had little desire to eat or speak to anyone. As I lay on my bed Mom came in and stared at me with a puzzled look. For a moment she just stood in the doorway looking. I was sure she could tell I was stoned out of my mind but I didn't care.

"I was going to ask why you do this to yourself, but I guess it wouldn't matter, would it?"

"No, it wouldn't," I replied.

"The Nichols family called earlier and wanted to know if you want to watch a movie with them. I told them that I'd make a French bread pizza that you could take up there," she said, closing the door.

"Thanks," I replied.

I decided perhaps that was where I needed to be at that moment. My self-esteem was just above bottom-dweller and I had no reason for staying in the house with Mom. I showered and got dressed, then saw that my face and skin again gave me away. But I didn't think either John or Darlene would recognize the tattletale signs of drug abuse. I convinced myself that I could pass it off as being tired.

As I rang the doorbell of the Nichols family's house I took a deep breath and hoped that they wouldn't notice anything wrong. Darlene opened the door and I handed her the pizza that Mom had made. She was glad to see me —as always—and invited me downstairs to watch a movie with the family.

John asked how school was going and if I was excited over graduating later in the week. I had forgotten about graduation, and pondered the thought as we watched the movie. I couldn't focus on the show, I was so preoccupied with the fact that I was about to graduate high school. Yet it didn't faze me in the least. All my life I had expected that when the day finally came, somehow I would be cleaned up and ready for the world.

And now look where you are, I thought. *You're strung out once again, and you're back to the same old routine of hiding it all from everyone.*

"What a loser"—only I failed to keep the thought in my head and spoke it out loud. "I was talking about the movie," I quickly added.

John and Darlene looked at each other like I was from another planet. At that moment I might as well have been.

I turned back toward the screen and tried to grasp some part of what was going on as quickly as I could. Once the show was over and it was well past the normal bedtime for the Nichols kids, I said my good-byes. I started to leave when Darlene asked me if everything was all right.

"I just have a lot on my mind right now," I said.

"Do you want to talk about it?" she asked.

I paused. I desperately wanted to say: "Where do I begin?" But as usual I just said: "It's just that Mom and I aren't getting along—again."

I knew that they would accept that response; it was the trump card I played whenever I needed to close the door on a conversation. Inside I wanted to spill my guts and have someone who cared for me reach out and simply hold me. I knew that at the age of eighteen it was kind of a silly thing to desire—but it was all I really wanted.

I could tell that Darlene wasn't convinced that there was nothing more to it than that. She asked if I wanted to come for dinner the next night. "Sure, thanks," I gratefully said.

The walk home was less than two minutes and I dreaded the thought of going there. It was just past eleven. As I approached the front door, I could hear Mom and Scott arguing over something. They were arguing like we used to. I stepped back off the porch and walked down the street to the corner just a few houses away, then down a few more streets. Without thinking about it, I found myself passing by Cindy's house—Cindy was one of the girls I had been with at a few of the parties before I went to Hawaii. Just then she flew out of the front door and slammed it behind her, screaming some profanity at her father. We were both surprised to see each other. She came over and walked with me down the street.

Very little was said between us as we walked. I knew that she had issues at home and she knew I had as well. Before long we were by the open fields behind some houses. We sat down on the embankment and I put my arm around her. Within a moment we started to kiss.

"Do me a favor," she said.

"What?" I asked.

"Can we go back to your room?"

I recalled the times before when Cindy and I snuck in the backyard and into my room at night. Since the room was directly off the back porch, it was easy to get in and out of.

"Yeah, sure, but we have to be quiet this time, my brother's still up," I said.

As we walked back to my street I pushed away the conflicting thoughts of trying to be a clean and decent teenager while at the same time being just a normal one. We still hardly spoke as we walked. We made it to the backyard, then, unnoticed, slipped into the room and turned off the lights. Once again I was trading what little innocence I had left for the secrets of the night.

A while later, I set the alarm to make sure we woke up before anyone else in the house did. It was almost three in the morning.

By the end of the week I was to graduate high school and move on with my life. Yet I still had no idea of who I was, what I was—or why I was even alive.

The day before graduation I found the opportunity to hang out with a few friends from high school and plan "the big graduation party."

I knew that before the end of the day I would feel the need to disconnect with my feelings and anxieties by getting high and drinking myself insane. There was just one thing that must be done before I could go to the party. Unlike many of the other kids I hung out with, I knew the value of a diploma. But I couldn't attend the last day of school to receive it if I wanted to be at the party.

The day before graduation I asked Darlene to pick up the diploma—because I would be "unavailable." I made up some excuse that made sense, and she agreed.

Little did I know that it would eventually lead me to almost exposing my life to the two people that I just couldn't possibly have disappointed and still have faced again.

When Friday arrived, I woke with a determination to destroy myself this time, to bury my feelings with as many drugs as it was possible to take. In the past, when the opportunity to get high presented itself, I would never turn it down. But this time it was different, and scary—I was planning it long beforehand. The desire wasn't new, but it was stronger than I ever remembered it: I wanted to get so insane and so high, like I had never been before.

Once I arrived at the school parking lot, it took no time to locate the kids I knew. We all hung out behind the gym near the football field, away from the main building. As I walked down the school hallway, I was struck by the exciting, festive atmosphere—it was everywhere. I don't think any senior attended a single class that day. The corridors were as full of kids as the parking lot was full of cars.

The excitement only added to my anticipation of getting high. Perhaps I had now evolved into an out-and-out drug addict.

I had never felt such anticipation as I did now. There was nothing that was going to stop me. I wanted to go as far over the edge as I could. I didn't want to think about the conflicts in my life—Mom, the lies I had told John and Darlene, or anything else. I was tired of carrying the conflict like a rock too heavy to dispose of.

By lunchtime we all were well on our way to being insanely high. I'd brought with me to the party what was left of my paycheck and was prepared to have the time of my life. The barbecue was cooking, the coolers were full of beer, and the counters were full of booze—and of course the bedroom was full of drugs.

Nathan Bennett was at the party, and that was all I needed. After all this time he and I still seemed to have the same agenda. We went together into the bedroom, but were disappointed at the familiar selection of options we found there. None of the drugs were enticing enough to just grab and use.

"Ever done this?" he said, holding out a bag.

"What is it?" I asked.

"You'll like it. It's like nothing you've ever done before."

It was as if he knew exactly what to say to me and, being in the mood that I was at that moment, all I could say was: "Where?"

I followed him out into the driveway and we got in his car. He retrieved a kit from the backseat and opened it. Before long he had pulled out two needles, melted the powder, and filled the syringes. Up to that point I had snorted, smoked, eaten, drunk, or just plain swallowed almost every drug I had heard of. I didn't press him on what it was we were about to take. I was more concerned about using a syringe than anything else.

I tied a small rubber tube around my arm to stop the blood flow for a moment, then pushed the needle just under the skin and into the vein that now protruded from my arm. Once the syringe was empty, I untied the tube and sat back.

Within a moment I felt the wrath of the fluid flowing up my arm and almost instantly started to feel different. The calmness and warmth I felt was by far the most outrageous as well as the most horrifying effect of any drug I had taken up to that point. I leaned over toward Nathan. As he fell back in the front seat, I asked: "What the hell is this?"

"It's heroin, stupid."

I was horrified.

I had never used a needle before. I had smoked heroin, but using a needle was too much for me. It was strong, it was deadly, it was addictive. And it was perfect.

I have no idea how long we sat there or what we talked about. I remember leaving the car and walking back to the house. With most other drugs I always felt either disoriented or completely separated from myself. But this was different: I knew exactly who I was and what I was doing. I was filled with an overwhelming feeling of comfort and ease with myself.

As we walked into the backyard, where the party was in full swing, we looked at each other as if we'd had the same idea at the same time. We walked straight over to the girls, parting the crowd that stood around them.

"*You guys are ripped!*" two of the girls said in unison.

Nathan looked at me again and I at him as we fed off each other. We each took one of the girls by the hand and went into the house. Behind us the small crowd cheered as they watched us walk away. I had an incredible sense of power and control. And it would last longer than with any heroin I'd used before.

Afterward, without hesitation I led the girl I'd been with outside—and grabbed a motorcycle. The feeling of freedom the bike and the high gave me was more than exciting. We rode around the area for a while before heading over to the school parking lot. By the end of the day we were back at the house and relaxing. The high had worn off. At first it didn't bother me that it, and the day, were over. I said my good-byes and left.

Once I was home I went to bed and slept for the rest of the evening. When I awoke, it hit me. I was exhausted and cold. As I lay there, I was shaking uncontrollably. My body was completely trashed. The feeling of sickness and lethargy that I was used to from other worn-off highs was not the same as I now felt. This was worse. All I could think about was the drug, how good it had made me feel and how bad I felt now. And how much I wanted more of it to make me feel better.

I didn't leave the house for a day and a half.

Once I was able to carry myself as normal, I made my way up to the Nichols house to inquire if Darlene had picked up my diploma. I took care to make sure that I looked almost presentable, not like death warmed over. I felt like it, but I didn't want to look like it.

Within a few minutes of arriving at their house, they informed me that Darlene had seen me riding around on a motorcycle at the very time I was supposed to be off doing the all-important errand I had told her about.

I had never thought it possible. The chances that she would be in the school grounds during the few minutes I'd spent there myself seemed more than unlikely. The odds against it were monumental, in fact, and yet it was just my luck. I didn't know what to say. I knew that I had been caught in another lie and that she was mad with me and disappointed. I was sure that this was the beginning of the end of her trust in me and of my secret life as well.

Darlene never really went into any detail about what she thought or what she understood about me after that. I believe that she had her suspicions, but kept them between herself and John. I hated the fact that I had disappointed them yet again. I had been well and truly busted, caught in the web I'd woven for myself. I was now on the verge of exposing what I'd spent years hiding—my total embarrassment over myself.

11

FORSAKEN?

Just before I turned eighteen I took a good hard look at myself.
I was fearless. I was emotionless. I held little concern for life. I
was, overall, dangerous. I would never fit in anywhere. I
tried to follow in Ross's footsteps and join the service.

I had made some very serious mistakes and had ruined
several chances to get my life in order. I knew the damage I
was capable of. I was afraid of myself—I mean really afraid
of myself. And I was going to leave that house if it killed
me—which would be fine with me.

FROM 1983 THROUGH 1986 I spent my time in southern California in the military. I joined the service in Salt Lake City and went directly into boot camp.

By 1986 I was more than aware that I wasn't cut out to be a soldier. Having served less than the standard three years, and with nowhere else to go, I returned home to Salt Lake City.

The people were different; the kids that once were everywhere to be seen in the neighborhood were now young adults. Fewer and fewer bicycles scattered the lawns. In just a few short years, the places and people I once knew had changed.

But it seemed as if, whereas everyone around me was different now, I was still the same.

I was devastated to learn that John, Darlene, and the kids had moved from Salt Lake and were now living in Richmond, Virginia. Judy Prince had given me their address and phone number when she told me about their move. It seemed that John had been offered a much better job in Richmond, and he took it.

The days passed by without much to report; Mom and Scott left me to my own devices and I could come and go as I wished.

I had thought about writing to John and Darlene and asking if I could move out there and start over, but it was hard to admit that I was getting nowhere and afraid to be on my own. By all appearances I was a twenty-one-year-old adult, but on the inside I was still that rebellious teenager struggling to find myself.

With all the courage I could muster I sent a letter to Darlene, asking if they would consider allowing me to move out there temporarily until I was able to make it on my own. It was my last hope.

As day followed day I became increasingly depressed. I knew that either they never got the letter, or they did and wanted no part of me—just like everyone and everything else in my life. I'd messed up the chances I'd had to open up to John and Darlene. I was done—I was beaten.

In a matter of weeks I was back to my old self, strung out worse than I had ever been. I was beyond reckless. I was more dangerous to myself than ever.

I was an angry and suicidal young man.

I chased that smoking dragon, heroin, and I grew to hate it. I now faced the biggest conflict I had ever faced or have faced since. I just didn't care about me, or anyone else.

If John and Darlene didn't want me around and had somehow found out from Mom what my life was really like, it was over. I couldn't live with the knowledge that John and Darlene and the kids knew about my lifestyle *and* that they had been kept out of it deliberately.

I was just too ashamed to think about what Mom might have told them before they left the neighborhood.

Thankfully I found my youngest brother Keith untouched by the disease that plagued our family. He was now sixteen and struggling with Mom to get his driver's license, just as I had struggled. I knew Mom had backed off as far as her abusive drunken tendencies. She was getting just too old for it now—she was nearly fifty-eight.

Her mind had slipped even farther away than when I had last been there. She was almost a different person in the same skin. She looked the same—facial expressions, clothes, hair, drinking habits—only now she'd completely forgotten the last ten years or so.

Here I was once again back at the very place I'd grown to hate, in that house and with the people that I just couldn't relate to, and the Nichols family had moved. Rob and Judy Prince were still there, but Rob had become very involved in his legal career and didn't seem to want me around as much. Judy was always just as helpful and down to earth as I knew her to be. The last thing I wanted was to cause any issues between Rob and Judy, so I distanced myself from them as well.

The weeks passed, and I found that my first impression had been right—most of the friends I had in high school had disappeared. One of the girls I used to hook up with had a daughter and was working to support the two of them. The carefree party environment I had left behind was gone.

Life had really changed. It was becoming real, and it scared me. I had no career and no real family—in fact, I was left living with the remnants of a real-life Addams family.

I had to get out, and fast. I didn't know how or where to, only that if I didn't I would end up a junkie, in jail, or as a father living in some white-trash trailer park.

I took another meaningless job at Ryan Steakhouse and worked as much as I could just to be out of the house. I would occasionally score some drug or drink myself stupid or find a girl I used to know and have some emotionless sex.

I had no direction: no support, no desire to get ahead, and no one to share anything with. I was completely alone. Life could not have seemed more pointless.

Eventually I snapped. And I made a decision: at least I wanted Darlene to know what I was going through. I sat in my bedroom one evening and wrote the letter. I was just the same, and my life was going nowhere, I told her. I was just spinning wheels and not getting anywhere. I had no reason or desire to do anything. I felt so alone. Again, I danced around the possibility of me moving to Richmond to be with them.

As the days turned to weeks I began to lose hope. I believed that it just wasn't going to happen. I became yet more depressed and found myself at the bottom of many of the same old highs. I was spiraling downward fast.

Then it happened: a letter arrived. I knew it was Darlene—her handwriting was unique. I took the letter out of the mailbox and sat on my bed for a half hour before I opened it. I just couldn't take the rejection, if that was what was in there. With both reluctance and anticipation I opened the letter—and found the same old Darlene that I knew before. They'd had a family meeting with all of the kids. John and Darlene had agreed to have me come out and live with them until I got on my feet, both emotionally and financially.

I was about to leave it all behind.

I was convinced that I could now open my heart. I was sure that John and Darlene would understand now. Maybe they could even look past it all and see me for what I wanted to be—*normal*.

I made the arrangements to fly out with just the few things I had. The airfare fit right into my budget: less than a few hundred dollars—it was all I had left. I didn't have much that reminded me of my childhood, after what I had sold for drugs or tossed out. I had one small suitcase, one small box of keepsakes, and the clothes on my back. I purchased the ticket and announced that I was going to Virginia.

Surprisingly, Mom was actually hopeful for me. "I hope you do get your life in order, Richard. I hope you find what you've been looking for," she said.

That was the only conversation I had with Mom that I really believed she was sincere about and able to fully comprehend. It was the time I most felt it might be possible to begin repairing our relationship and finally overcome the hate, the fear, and the regret. It was also the last time I would see her alive.

Had I known this during that moment I had with Mom that *didn't* end with me being hurt, demoralized, or degraded, I would have said so much more to her. Looking back, though, I know that neither of us would have been able to say what was really on our minds—Mom because she didn't recall much of the last decade, me because I wasn't ready to actually let her go once and for all.

When the plane landed just outside Richmond, I was anxious and nervous. Once I got off the plane and saw the two of them waiting for me at the end of the ramp, I could barely contain myself. I was happy to see John. I'd always had respect for him and his commitment to himself and his family. He was always kind and gentle toward me. I'm sure that most people were intimidated by his size when they first saw him. At well over six feet tall and over two hundred and fifty pounds, he carried himself well, but all the same his size made me feel slightly afraid.

But it was Darlene who was my real savior. From the first day I met her she had never been anything but sincere and so easy to talk to. She always made me feel like I was one of her sons. I never told her that in many ways I considered her my mommy.

Now I had another chance to share my feelings and open up to not only John and Darlene, but also Wendy who was now fifteen, Steve (fourteen), Heidi (twelve), Heather (eight), and Adam and Amy who were now five. It was the perfect family setting. I had the chance to be a big brother and make sure that Steve didn't make the same mistakes I'd made, and to have sisters that I had never had. After twenty-one years I had finally found my place. What I didn't expect was to find that in many ways I was far behind Wendy and Steve emotionally.

I settled in with Steve—we were sharing a room together. Neither of us had much stuff to call our own, but we had all we needed. The first few days were the hardest for me. I quickly found out that my body had to adjust more than I did. The weeks before I moved out I had spent what little money I had on crack cocaine or heroin. I hadn't heard from Darlene yet, and I was sure at the time that she had written me off just like I thought everyone else had. I was depressed and exhausted. The few days I had to clean up my act really didn't catch up with me until I arrived in Richmond.

And the first few nights were incredibly hard. It got so bad that at one point I lay in bed awake and shook. I couldn't eat. But I wasn't about to tell either John or Darlene what the real issue was. I was so embarrassed about it that I sweated it out rather than reveal just how self-destructive I had been.

Not long after this, John made it clear to Steve and me that the bedroom window was to remain closed at night, as he didn't want to heat all of Richmond. I tried my best to keep the window closed, but I convinced Steve to open it after we were in bed. It was the only way I could both cool off and breathe. During the day I would lie low and simply say I was tired. No one must know that in reality I was withdrawing from the weeks of day-after-day drug abuse. At one point, just before Darlene's letter arrived, I had kept the same high going for several days, happy with being comfortably numb.

John reminded me a few times that he'd asked that the windows remain closed, but I kept on opening them anyway.

Then one night he came into the room with a hammer and a few nails in his hands. My first reaction when I saw the hammer was pure flashback. Many times, Mom had come into my room as I slept and struck out at me with whatever she had in her hand at the time. I was paralyzed with fear.

As if in slow motion, John was coming farther into the room. It seemed like it took forever for him to pass the foot of my bed and continue over to the window. John's size, him being annoyed at me, and the flashes from my past combined to convince me that I was right back in Daly City, in my bed, as Mom walked in the room.

He wasn't going to ask again, John said. Since neither Steve nor I would listen, he was going to take care of it himself. He simply nailed the window shut, and walked out.

I looked at Steve and he looked at me. I could tell that he was shocked, though for a different reason than I was. Steve was shocked that his father had reacted that way. I was shocked that he'd reacted *only* that way. All I could think about as he walked across the floor to the window was the sort of sudden unpredictable reactions I'd been so accustomed to from Mom, that usually ended up in me getting badly hurt. I should have known that John would never have been able to hurt his kids in any way like Mom did. I should have known that he would never have harmed me, either.

For the first time since I was that little redheaded freckle-faced boy, in the days when my brother David, not me, was the target of Mom's vicious outbursts, I felt like I was home. I felt like I *had* a home. This was the first of the thousands of lessons I learned as the seventh son.

12

TROOP NICHOLS

The opportunity to see and experience a family as they went about their day-to-day lives was incredible. Not many twenty-two-year-olds have the chance, let alone the desire, to be around a family of kids ranging from six to sixteen years old. I loved it.

I also learned fast that jealousy is very hard to overcome. Up to now I had been angry, in many ways fearless, ignorant, and self-serving. I had never had any reason to be jealous, anyone to be jealous of. It was devastating to accept that I was now jealous of a handsome, popular, outgoing teenager who was seven years my junior. Steve Nichols taught me a great deal about confidence, pride, and humor. Despite our age difference, we enjoyed each other's company. Not only did he help me as a friend, he also helped me as a brother—a real brother.

STEVE WAS DIFFERENT. Not only was he confident like his sister Wendy, he was also cool and collected. He had the looks, the personality, and the charm. He had everything I ever wanted, yet I felt I had nothing I could offer *him*.

Once I settled in and became comfortable with being in a busy household full of kids, I grew to like Steve even more. Between Scouts, music, dances, soccer, band, school, and a social life that I always wished I had, the kids were busier than time allowed for.

Steve always made me feel like a big brother; of course, having a driver's license made it a little easier for a fifteen-year-old to like me.

It was Steve who started me off on a love of music. He was my introduction to some of the many different bands I grew to like. And for the first time I was becoming aware of my appearance, because Steve's appearance was very important to him—as you'd expect in any normal young man. I was becoming concerned over hygiene, my hair, my use of current slang, and of course, my clothes.

In 1987, and at the age of twenty-two, this was all new to me. But before long I was spending my time, and what little money I had from my job at a local restaurant, on records (LPs) and parachute pants. Whenever I was able, I bought gifts for Steve: clothes, burgers, records, concert tickets. I loved sharing with him. In many ways he was my unspoken hero. I could never say that to him. I couldn't let him or anyone know that I was that self-conscious.

One of the few times I was ever really mad at Steve was right after I had worked many extra hours to acquire some much coveted Depeche Mode tickets. It was one of the bands Steve and I really liked and both wanted to see. For weeks we wondered if we would get to go to the concert, how we would ever afford the eighty dollars. Little did he know that I had planned on taking him and was already working hard to afford the tickets. Eventually, the day came and I had them in my hand. We marveled at the chance to see the band. We spent most of the next few days talking about what they would be like and what songs they would open with; sleep meant little to us.

The night before the concert Steve had done something wrong. I don't recall exactly what, but I do know that John and Darlene were justified in grounding him for such a stupid act, whatever it was.

So there I was holding a pair of tickets to one of the best and biggest shows in Richmond, Virginia, and now I was going alone. We had both looked forward to that day for weeks, and now I was mad as hell at him. I couldn't believe he would be so selfish as to risk being punished on the eve of the big event.

I didn't want to go without him. I could have easily called one of the friends I had that were much closer to me in age—Ron, Chris, or Geoff. Chris and Geoff were brothers and had been friends with Ron for a number of years before

I knew any of them. They usually hung out together and spent time watching movies.

Ron was the one that I grew close to quickly. He hardly ever asked me about my family back home. He knew I was living with John and Darlene and the kids as another son.

I really enjoyed the Datsun 280Z sports car he and his father had. Bright yellow and with more power and thrust than any car should be allowed to have, that car gave Ron and me more fun than we would have thought possible. Ron just wanted a friendship and so did I—just a friend my own age, someone who didn't know about me and what I had been through. It wasn't hard dodging his occasional questions about my background.

It didn't take me long to realize that Ron, Chris, and Geoff had had little or no exposure to, or experience with, drugs and alcohol. The slightest reference to getting "high" or "drunk" was taken as a stretch of the imagination, not an actual desire.

Often Ron would call on a Friday night asking what I was doing or what I wanted to do. My replies, always similar, became a standing joke. Most of the time I simply said: "We can get stoned," or "We could find a bar somewhere."

Ron usually laughed it off and made some more realistic suggestion as to how to spend our evenings. He had no idea of what I had made of myself over the last eight years, and that's exactly what I wanted. No one to know.

———————

Ron or Chris would have loved to go to the Depeche Mode concert with me, but it wouldn't have been the same without Steve. So I did the only thing I could. I gave the tickets to one of Steve's friends who, like most people in town, hadn't been able to get any. I told him that Steve wanted him to have them: "Steve isn't able to go and he thought of you. So here you go. Enjoy!"

Inside it killed me, but then again, I felt pretty good that I had a true friend and a brother all in one. I ended up staying at home and hanging around the house with him, miserable and mad as hell at John and Darlene for grounding him. We made the best of it and we all survived.

———————

Steve had a circle of friends his own age, and *some* of them were boys. By the age of fifteen, like most boys, he had shown an interest in girls. I could tell that Steve loved his sisters very much and he would stand up for them without fear or favor. But they were, after all, *sisters;* in his eyes, they weren't real girls. Steve already had an eye for the girls.

He was involved in soccer and was more than good at it. Once I tried to act the big brother and demonstrate my superior agility. But I quickly learned that he could run, kick, and dodge way better than I could—he could run circles around me, in fact. Occasionally, I would go to a match with

John to watch Steve play. John was very proud of his son's ability and his sportsmanship. I, on the other hand, couldn't fall over a soccer ball if I tried. It didn't bother me that Steve was athletic, until it struck me that there were so many things that Steve was that I wasn't.

By the time I had been there less than a year, he had so many friends, and in particular so many girlfriends, that I felt like a fifth wheel. Through no fault of his, I started to become jealous of his popularity. I was feeling out of place, and I knew the age difference was significant. It's one thing when *you're* the teenager and your brother is just a kid. It's okay to be a teenage dork, even. But when you are twenty-two and your younger brother is the popular teen, it's hard being the dork.

Steve tried to make me feel comfortable, but it became apparent that he wanted his own space. I just couldn't get over the fact that he was where I'd wanted to be years earlier. I started to question my place in life once again. But I had to face the fact that my chances to be a kid were long gone. I had to grow up. I knew in my heart that the teenager within me, even if that teenager had never thrived, was grown up now, and I had to allow myself to be an adult.

John and Darlene were supportive of my quest to grow up and act like an adult. They helped me understand that the more I acted like an adult, the more I would be treated like one. I learned, among other things, to balance my checkbook—and hated everything about that particular lesson. It took me a long time to understand that just because I had checks left in my checkbook, it didn't mean I had the money to cover them. Paying bills was a chore and seemed like a waste of money for me. I could easily have found much better use for and more fun things to do with the little money I was earning at the restaurant.

At least I found that as I separated myself from Steve and spent more time with guys my own age, Steve still enjoyed my company. He was still the little brother I knew. I came to realize that the time I spent worrying about being a loner was a waste. I did have friends my own age, *and* I was still close to my new younger brother, Steve. I had been drug-free for over a year and was enjoying true friendships with guys who were not there to support my egocentric paranoia, and who liked me not for my ability to smoke myself into the Stone Age, but for other reasons. Finally, and most important, I had a family.

And I even looked better; my skin was clear and I didn't look like death warmed over. I could actually breathe; I smelled good, I looked good—and I almost felt good about myself.

One of the few people who have ever touched my soul was Heather Nichols. She had the ability to talk to me in the innocence of youth, and yet she had desires and emotions equal to my own. In many ways we were a lot alike, looking for ourselves among the crowd of kids that surrounded us. We both wore our feelings on our sleeves, but found it incredibly hard to communicate exactly what we really felt— except to each other. Inside we had issues in our own minds and in our own hearts, and we understood the difference.

It was as if emotionally we were the same, the only difference between us being that I was almost twenty-three and she was coming up for ten.

Of all the kids and all the different personalities that made up the Nichols home, Heather was the one that I wanted to understand the most. I thrived on her ability to express herself. As with most nine-year-olds, she often didn't know what it was she wanted or needed, but she was able to talk to me in such a real and honest way. I wished I had been like her at that age.

I guess throughout my short years with the Nichols family, I always thought of myself at different stages when I looked at Heather. I could relate to what she felt inside, even though the confusion and unsorted feelings were caused by such different events in our lives. Of course, she was oblivious to how I knew of the importance of sharing your feelings. She just did it because it was part of her style. It had taken me years and years to get to that point, and she was already there at the age of not quite ten.

About the same time I was having those issues with Steve and becoming aware that I had to grow up and be my own person, Heather taught me something that made the transition from teenager to adulthood meaningful. As we talked about everything from having a "dumb younger brother and mean older sisters" to the feeling we sometimes shared that "no one loves or understands me," I realized that she had no idea of just how innocent her world was. She never knew anything of this at the time. She had no fears of sleeping at night, no fears of being hurt or belittled beyond ridicule. She certainly couldn't comprehend one symptom of the fear and pain I carried around: oftentimes I would catch myself crying as we talked. It just touched me so much that a child could be that innocent and think the world was falling down around her when in reality she was free as a bird.

The biggest concern she had was the normal rivalry of siblings. I reminded her that her brother and sister, Steve and Wendy, loved her and didn't *mean* to be older—they just were. Being the middle child, she had her share of being stepped on and over, but she never knew just how good she had it.

Heather had no problem speaking her mind or sharing her feelings with me. Often we would sit together on the back porch. She was able to talk to me as an older brother and as an adult as well. I had to hold back my true feeling that her concerns about being "lost in the crowd," real as they were, were actually a blessing, and something I had always coveted.

So many times I wanted to just reach out and hug her, and cry with her. I wanted to just let it all out as she did so many times. I so desperately wanted to cry as a child would, as Heather did. In many ways I envied her the luxury of being able to talk. I recalled so many times when I was her age, having such a fear of adults that I stuttered constantly. I couldn't string two words together, and yet here she was talking to me and sharing her feelings and letting me help her sort them out. In so many ways I wanted to be Heather, to relive my early years all over again. If she'd had her way we would have traded places. Or rather, truth be known, if I'd had *my* way, we would have.

Each time I sat and talked with her, I got a little closer to understanding myself. The feelings I'd had as a kid were so opposite to what Heather was going through that it made the difference as clear as day. Whereas I learned from Steve and Wendy the importance of being oneself, I grew to understand childhood through the eyes and heart of Heather Nichols.

I learned from Heather the importance of being a child.

———

The person that was the easiest to appreciate and get to know was Wendy. I had known her as a small child, but now that she was sixteen, she was very much her own person. She had a good sense of what was right and what was wrong. Her desire to embrace music and to achieve above average marks in school made her the brainiac of the family group. She had a sense of pride that I could only dream of.

Heidi, at the age of thirteen, was also easy to talk to. She was just getting out of the awkward preteen years and into the *really* awkward teenage ones. She had the ability to charm when she wanted to, and to stand up for herself when the occasion demanded.

The two girls were opposites. They needed each other, and yet were rivals. Their relationship reminded me of the one I always wanted Scott and me to have. We had our own issues with each other, and Wendy and Heidi Nichols did too. But Wendy and Heidi cared for each other, like sisters do. Heidi would never admit it out loud, but they needed each other both as sisters and as friends.

Wendy was able to make achieving one success after another look easy—it came natural to her. Her confidence and her desire to learn more and more were fueled by the support of her parents and a belief in herself. She went in for more activities than I can remember, and appeared to enjoy making order out of chaos. Heidi thrived on chaos, too.

Heidi was also an actress waiting to blossom. I would marvel at her ability to turn on the charm, and at her refusal to give in, no matter what the issue.

I had never really, deeply, loved anyone before. There were people that I enjoyed being around—and yes, people that I loved. But not like the twins, Adam and Amy. They taught me the meaning of brother-and-sisterly love.

They were the same age I was when my life was just starting to be a living nightmare. But Adam and Amy were so far from what I was when I was six years old. I loved being around them. I loved their freedom and their love of life. Often, when I thought of Adam, I thought of myself at that age. I so wished I'd had his love for life. But I couldn't allow anyone to know that Adam was so special to me. Without knowing my background, it would have been just too odd to understand. I saw in Adam everything I'd wanted to be. I saw in him the little boy I never could be.

When I arrived at the Nichols home, Adam and Amy were five years old. They soon became the high point of any day for me. They were loving and carefree and I envied their innocence and the internal beauty they showed me.

They were also my safety valve. Whenever I felt sorry for myself, or felt like I was not moving along at the pace I should be, I would spend as much time with them as I could. They were able to remind me of what life should have been like for me at that age. I was so excited to watch them learn to express themselves and be comfortable as the children they were. They had no fear of anything. They were real and they were tender.

Adam and Amy were the reason I finally became comfortable with the notion of being a father. I thought a lot about eventually having kids, and wanted so desperately for my own kids to love me like they did. I was convinced that someday, when I got myself together, I would be a father and my kids would be just as beautiful as Adam and Amy, both on the inside and on the outside.

Just as I did from the rest of the Nichols family, I learned a great deal from those two. I learned how to be patient and how to love life as they did. (One of my few disappointments to do with this period of my life would be to miss them growing up.)

Secretly I struggled with the overwhelming questions:

Could I ever be a parent?

What if what Mom did to us was out of my control and was a part of me that I had yet to discover?

Was I going to be an abusive parent?

Walking Adam and Amy down the street in a twin stroller, listening to them talking to each other though not really understanding too much of what they were saying, I began to see that fatherhood was perhaps a dream for me. Something I wanted, and yet something I was not sure I could ever achieve. I knew that anyone could be a father. The dream was to be looked up to like I looked up to John and to be respected and truly loved like I loved Darlene.

Adam and Amy helped me realize that even the most seemingly out-of-reach dreams can come true, if you truly want them to.

13

JOHN AND DARLENE

*John and Darlene, in their early forties, were more loving
than I, at the age of twenty-three, could comprehend. They
loved life, they loved each other, and they loved their kids.
But what shocked me the most was that they loved me: they
actually loved me. John and Darlene nurtured and taught
me as only a mother and father can do.*

*Darlene was the one that eventually got through that
thick layer I created on the surface. She had something that
I never did. She had real faith in herself, her husband, her
children, and God.*

JOHN AND DARLENE WORKED hard to keep the
kids happy and clothed. I truly felt that having one
more—me—wasn't going to make much difference. John
worked long hours and weekends, but he always managed to
find time for the kids and for others, too.

Since I never really had one before John, it's hard for me to define a father figure. He was strong and yet gentle, firm in his beliefs yet flexible in his judgment.

I have only a few select memories of my real father's face. I spent most of my young life without a father. John's fatherly love for his family was so foreign to me that I had to work to understand it. He tried hard to treat me like one of the kids. Inside, though, I was scared. He intimidated me. I wanted never to disappoint him, and to earn his respect. I know that oftentimes I fell short.

I loved my real father—he was my father.

But I loved John Nichols—he was my dad.

One of the mistakes I made during that time was not making that perfectly clear to John. Even to this day, I haven't. Had I not been so angry at the drastic difference between my real father and my dad, perhaps I would have been able to share that. John's ability to guide and support my emotional and spiritual growth was special to me.

But if there was one person who really saved me, it was Darlene. She taught me about self-respect, respect for my body as well as my mind. Her lessons, either by commission or omission, were always right on target. Her love for her children and her love for life were what I needed to see as a young man. She taught me so much more in the few short years I lived with the Nichols family than I had ever learned from my real mom.

Sometimes I talked to John and Darlene about my goals and what I wanted to do with my life.

———————

I had been working at a Ford truck dealership with Ron. For a while I enjoyed the company and the work. But as always I needed a better-paying job. The Ford Pinto I was driving at the time was falling apart and I just couldn't keep it running on the salary I had. I took another job, a better-paying one, as a parts delivery boy at another Ford dealership.

As I started to befriend some of the other guys my own age at the dealership, I quickly realized that I had to be strong in my resolution to remain drug- and alcohol-free. Many times after work some of the guys would go out for beers and we would go bowling. The temptations that I was exposing myself to were the worst part of being in that setup. I knew exactly what they were talking about each Monday after a weekend of getting high, drinking, and picking up girls. On the one hand I wanted to join them and smoke myself into the Stone Age again, and on the other I wanted no part of it. I wish I could say that the temptations went away and I overcame the desire, but the only thing I overcame was my sitting on the fence.

———————

Richmond had several churches that were attended by young single adults only. They were designed to help people with the same beliefs and values to share and grow together. Some members went to the services or functions only on rare occasions. I could tell that sometimes they felt comfortable with their peers and other times they didn't. I understood what they were feeling. As the weeks went by, I made a friend of one of the girls who had lived a lot like I had done. We talked and exchanged our memories of the good and the bad in that reckless lifestyle.

But the struggle to stay clean and drug-free ended up a losing battle for me.

Ron and Chris had been actively after me to go dancing with some girls they knew, and being as tempted as I was to go over the edge, I thought it a good idea and a safe place for me to be. So I agreed.

When I turned into the parking lot that evening, I saw that it was full, so I had to park around the back. Behind the dance hall, just a few yards away, was the house of one of the kids I worked with at the dealership. As I parked the car, he called out to me and invited me to the party that was going on at his house with his brother and a few girls they knew.

I turned and looked back at the hall, and felt that old feeling of confusion I knew so well. The decision I made that night was one of my worst.

I walked across the hall lawn, up the driveway, and into the house, then closed the door, leaving Ron and Chris wondering what had happened to me.

Within a few hours I was drunk and stoned out of my mind. But I wanted to be polite. I wanted no one to know that I thought the drugs at the party were too simple for me, childish. As usual, though, my mouth failed to obey my mind, and I made such a big deal about the choice of drugs.

"These are ridiculous. Don't you have any real drugs?" I said.

It took all of about two seconds for me to see that I was out of control and making an ass of myself.

When the morning light reached the bedroom I was sleeping in and I realized that the girl next to me was a total stranger, I panicked. I knew where I was and yet I didn't recall anything.

I gathered my clothes, but couldn't find my contact lenses. I knew that I couldn't drive without them, but I had to leave that house as soon as I could and make my way back home.

I spent the whole of the drive back thinking about what I would say to John and Darlene. They would be concerned if they knew that Ron and Chris had seen me pull into the parking lot, then not seen me again.

Darlene opened the back door before I could reach for the handle. The expression on her face changed from worry to disappointment the minute she saw me. I looked hungover, and I was. I looked like I'd slept in my clothes and I stank of smoke and booze.

The one person that I always wanted to make happy and whose confidence in me I was desperate to hang on to, was now seeing just what I was capable of—still—and how easily I could be tempted. It took a long time to live through the disappointment and the embarrassment. I vowed that I would never place myself in that position again. I'd learned that I still wasn't able to handle temptation.

It was several weeks before Darlene talked to me again like she used to. I felt her disappointment, and I understood it. I was crushed and embarrassed, and so was she. I had to accept that I had limitations, and I had to not only accept them but live with them, too. For the first time I sat down and took an inventory not only of what and who I wanted to be, but of who and what I couldn't be.

I'll never forget the disappointment on Darlene's face that morning. I vowed to always think of it when I needed a reason to turn around and walk the other way.

14

ON MY OWN

The three hardest years of my life—odd though this may seem—were between the ages of twenty-four and twenty-seven. I wasn't a child. I wasn't a teenager. But I wasn't yet a man, either. I still didn't know who or what I was. I was a tardy teenager, lost somewhere in the middle.

I was on my own and responsible for my actions, and for myself. I was truly alone. But it was the beginning of the change.

I T H A D B E E N N E A R L Y three years since I'd moved out of the Nichols family's home. They had moved to another state, and the few friends that I'd made were off to college. I was left to figure it all out. I hadn't spoken to Mom or any of my brothers for a couple of years.

It hadn't been difficult, being on my own. I was working at a state job in Richmond as a weights and measures inspector for the Department of Agriculture. It was a basic nine-to-five job. There was nothing special about what I did. There was nothing special about myself, either. The constant reminder that my friends were off at college was aggravating. There was little chance of me getting into college. Despite all the love and care I'd received from Darlene and John, from the whole family, I didn't have the self-esteem to even try.

I started to see more of one of the girls I had met at a singles gathering, and it wasn't long before Jennifer and I were spending most evenings together. Being introduced to her family was difficult. I found that I really didn't fit in. I had no family nearby, and my real one wasn't a good topic for conversation. Jen's parents thought it odd that I never talked about my family. Whenever they planned a family event, they would ask if I wanted to join in.

I learned a lot from Jen; I learned that honesty really is the best policy and that if you are going to build a real relationship there cannot be any secrets. But I couldn't open up and share what I was before we met. Unfortunately, we didn't last that long.

We had a normal platonic relationship. Often I would sleep over in a separate room after a long movie or after spending time together. Jen would get up for work, and I would leave as she did, for my job.

One evening after we'd all gone to bed, her father, Buddy, checked on the two of us. I was in the guest room sound asleep, and Jen was in her bedroom. As Buddy opened the door to the room, I sat bolt upright in bed, and as he opened the door farther, I moved away from him. His reaction to this behavior was more than surprise. He was shocked that I could jump from asleep to awake in a split second, simply from the sound of the door opening.

There were other oddities that I know Jen's parents noticed, but never said anything about. They just kept Jen close and safe. It was almost like they were searching for the real me, just as I was.

One night when Jen and I went to our separate rooms, I was upset. We had been spending more and more time together. I was becoming emotionally involved, and I was afraid. From the moment my head hit the pillow, all I could think about was how to tell Jen and her parents about me and my past. They deserved to know who I really was and what I was going through.

At some point during the night, I had gotten out of bed and found a dark corner of the room to sit in. I was curled up in a fetal position, wearing only my briefs and a blanket, and with my head right in the corner.

Suddenly I heard the sound of creaking hinges, and the door opened. I knew it was Buddy checking on me. I could see him out of the corner of my eye. I felt ashamed as he came over to me. When he knelt down and asked me if I was all right, I didn't know what to say. How could I explain that I was so afraid of becoming involved with Jennifer that I must have gotten out of bed and crawled in the corner while I was asleep?

It was one of the many times I wanted to just evaporate away and not have to explain myself. It was also one of the most embarrassing moments I had ever experienced.

———————

There was just nothing I could offer Jen. I simply couldn't open up to her or her mother and father. I still didn't know what I wanted in life, nor did I have any real expectations of myself. It was pretty clear that I was just floating through life from one day to the next, and Jen wanted much more from her boyfriend than that. Her parents wanted much more from me, too. I wasn't willing, or able, to get myself together.

I had never been in love. At that point in my life, love had little value for me. I enjoyed the company of a girlfriend, and the experiences I had were all lessons learned, but I wasn't ready to share with anyone.

When Jen told me she wanted more from a relationship than I was able to provide, a stronger commitment, I took it as the inevitable other shoe dropping. It wasn't surprising that she wanted out. At the age of twenty-five, I knew I still needed to grow up. But it was more than a question of maturity, much more.

The trouble was I didn't know what I had to do to really change. Most of my life up to that point, whenever I needed to make a change all I did was change location, friends, or jobs. I never actually sat down and thought about changing *me;* changing what was inside and the way I thought and felt about myself.

It took the loss of a real girlfriend for me to begin to have a good look at myself. After Jen, after being alone for several months—by choice and design—I was able to focus on myself at my own pace.

The people I worked with knew little about me, too. When I thought about it, I could see there was almost no one around who knew anything about me: where I grew up, my family, my education, or any detail that made me different than anyone else. I was no one, in the middle of nowhere. It didn't matter what state I lived in or what friends I had. If I chose to keep myself distant from those around me, then I was alone. I was alone in the middle of the crowd: lost in a shuffle of day-to-day life, with no direction.

About six months after Jen said good-bye for the last time, my upstairs neighbor and I started to see a bit more of each other. Up till then, I used to sit outside on my front porch and watch the sunset, and she would watch it from hers.

I found it easy to be cordial and polite with no hidden agenda, no trying to impress or find some spark. So the day I discovered my neighbor, Lara, was interested in more than a friendly hello from me, I made the decision to stay out of a relationship until I was ready to truly share in one.

It was easy. All I had to do was say "no." That simple word is what kept me from continuing to wonder about whether to or not. I actually felt good about saying hello when I saw her out on her porch, knowing that we were still friends and yet only friends. That is what I had missed out on. I'd never opened up or shared anything with anyone one to one, even when I *thought* I was in a relationship. A real relationship takes so much more. I was never able to get past the maturity barrier I'd kept from my childhood.

I *wanted* to find someone to confide in, but it was just too much for me. As Lara shared more and more with me about herself, it felt so odd that I couldn't advance on what she already knew about me, which wasn't much at all. With my silence, I was keeping the necessary distance. On the one hand, I did want to open up and experience a real relationship based on more than physical attraction, based on trust and understanding. On the other hand, I knew that if I really shared what was in my heart, all the hurt and shame I still carried around with me, no one would want to be in a relationship with me. It was the most confusing and frustrating aspect of my young adult life.

I began to find ways to keep myself busy and at the same time to learn about *me*. I had no real idea what I liked to do, or what I didn't. When the summer of 1989 arrived, I decided to spend time at Virginia Beach, not far from Richmond. I spent as many weekends and nights there as I could. I was determined to become socially able, and I forced myself to say hello to people. Strange as it may sound, I'd never taken the chance to learn about being sociable. I was now beginning to feel confident enough to do just that.

It was that simple step of being alone *with a purpose* that made the change in me meaningful. In the past I had been alone by design, but without a reason. I'd failed to understand that I needed to feel good about myself before I could expect anyone else to like me. I had always believed that someday I would find someone who would change me and make me into the person I always wanted to be. What was missing from that notion was the fact that I didn't know who or what I was. How could I expect anyone else to like what might not even be there?

When I finally realized that I'd held the key to growing up all along, I felt frustrated. It now seemed so simple: All I needed was time with me, my real self. No girlfriends to keep at a distance. It had been there all the time, the answer I was looking for.

It was the answer to that endlessly recurring, simple yet profound, question, the one I had avoided for twenty years: *Who am I?*

I said to myself: *I'm not that little redheaded boy that haunts my dreams.*

I'm not the shallow, quiet teenager.

I'm a man now.

Once I was able to let go of the teenager and my self-induced social void, I was able to design, to welcome, the new me. New clothes, new cologne, and a new haircut made a difference to the outside, but with the inside I had a little trouble. After I'd spent several nights sitting out on the porch thinking, Lara asked if she could help me with whatever was on my mind.

I was comfortable in telling her what I was doing and why, and she was able to help me find what I needed, to find ways of determining who I was. Being around people was the key. She suggested going to see movies at the theater rather than renting them and bringing them home. After several months of finding new ways to break down the wall I had built around me, I found that I enjoyed being around *me*.

I bought a set of golf clubs and walked the course with other players. Hours of conversation and enjoyment of the game helped me open up. I realized that I didn't actually need to share all of my secrets, all that I was ashamed of. For so long it was all I had to share—so I'd shared nothing. I'd kept myself distant and private. Now I had common experiences that helped me understand that I was *normal*. I was just as ordinary as the next guy.

I had been clean for two years and I felt good about myself. I knew how to be sociable, and I even looked good. I smelled good, wore cologne, and hair gel. I was proud of myself. I was really enjoying the new me.

The night Lara told me that she needed to confide in me, that she needed help with a personal issue, I was overwhelmed with pride. Someone that I was not sexually involved with wanted something from me, something from me that would be respected and appreciated. In fact, what I learned that night was difficult for me to believe.

She had to make a decision, she said. She had been seeing a young man and was torn between him and another. She was interested in this other guy, but he didn't seem to want anything from her. She enjoyed his company and conversation, but they had agreed they would only be friends. Yet she wanted more from him.

She had now found this other guy who was showing an interest in her, and she was torn between her feelings for the first guy and her feelings for the new one. I confessed that I had never been in such a position, but had the luxury of explaining that my hunch was that I would have to ask each of them separately what they felt.

"I can't," she said.

"Why not?"

"The first friend is the one that I really would like to be with, but I know he doesn't want to be with me," she confessed.

"How do you know what he wants? Have you asked him?" I asked.

"Not recently."

"I'm confused. How do you know that the first friend doesn't want to be with you if you haven't asked to be more than friends?" I asked her.

"You told me that from the beginning—remember?" she said boldly.

"Me? You want to be with me?"

I was shocked. The friend that I had opened up to, in whom I'd confided that I had no idea who I was and whose help I had asked for—the one who had helped me start to find myself—was now asking me to be more than casual friends.

It was the first time since the Nichols family that I felt someone liked me for me. She knew I was lost and yet she wanted to help. She knew I was just finding myself and couldn't offer anything in return.

"I don't understand," I said.

"I don't, either," she confessed. "All I know is that I like you for being you. You're honest and you're not afraid of your feelings."

I realized that she was sincere. She really liked me.

"I have to confess, this is the first time I've thought twice about something like this. Don't get me wrong—I think you're pretty and I like you," I said. "I just think I'm better off finding myself right now."

As we talked, I realized that I was so much further ahead than I'd thought. I was able to think through a future relationship and accept the fact that I wasn't ready for it. When the time came, I wanted more from a relationship than I had gotten in the past. I wanted more from myself and more from my partner. I wanted a real and loving togetherness. Yes, part of me wanted more from Lara than just a "casual" friendship. But I wanted to find myself first even more.

We decided to talk more about it another time. I spent that night alone in my room thinking about the girl in the apartment upstairs. I was now seeing her in a different way: I never *had* thought of her as anything other than a friend.

That's it, I thought.

That's what was missing.

It must have been two in the morning when I rang her bell. When she saw it was me, she opened the door and invited me in. She knew I was there to say something important, and I knew what I had to do. She took my hand, walked me over to the couch, and waited for what I had to say. She was wearing a filmy negligee. It was difficult to focus on what I needed to tell her, but it was rewarding to be able, at the same time, to see beyond the physical and experience the sharing of feelings and the emotions of a real friendship.

"You've helped me in ways that I'm just realizing now. You're a real friend," I said. "I can't risk changing that, yet I know that by saying this, I'll force you to move on."

We talked, and she made me feel that I had value and worth. A few cups of coffee later, at sunrise, I left her apartment feeling as I had never felt before in that situation. It was the first time I'd walked away.

I felt something I hadn't in years: pride. I felt like a man. I was in control of myself and what I said. It felt wonderful to feel real.

I expected a certain awkwardness when I saw her out on the porch after that. But on the contrary, she helped me learn more about what it was to be friends. Not that we didn't find humor in the sadness of our being only friends.

We talked more and more as friends, in particular about what she was experiencing with her new boyfriend. I was excited to be able to help her and to express my thoughts and feelings. We would sit on her sofa and talk. Sometimes, when she was wearing her short pink negligee, it could be difficult. Often she would call me after I was already in bed. I would simply put on my shoes and go upstairs in whatever I was wearing, often just my pajama top and boxers.

It felt good to have such a friend. There was so much more to our relationship than just being each other's confidant, but I wish I had shared with her what I most wanted to, my past and who I really was. Looking back, though, I think she would have understood.

I was saddened the day she told me she was leaving the apartment complex. She'd decided to take her own advice and go back home and find herself. The morning she left she gave me a gift that only she could have given me.

"I'll miss you," she said.

I kissed her on the cheek and we held one another for a moment. What I felt then was more than I had ever expected to experience: I had a real friend.

It was the first time I'd had to let someone go that I cared about in this particular way. True, I'd let Ross, Dad, David, and the Prince and Nichols families go, but this was different. This was someone who had not only helped me with what I'd been struggling with—she was someone who wanted to be with me, yet allowed me my space. She was someone that I wanted to be with, yet I'd forced myself in one important respect to turn away from her. She could have been so much more to me, and yet she was all I needed at that point. She was a true partner that I let slip away.

I watched her drive away, then went back inside my apartment. I was on my own, and it felt great. I didn't need the memories I'd carried around with me. I didn't need the apparitions that shared my dreams any longer. I had been dependent on my past as the only way to understand myself, but now I was happy to try and rebuild my life.

I had come so far and I knew that I was close to being whole. I didn't want to change anything: our relationship, or anything about me. She was a wise and honest friend and confidante. I didn't want to ruin it.

15

LETTING GO . . . AGAIN

Christmas has always been a favorite time for me. The sounds and smells of the Christmas holidays have always made me feel like a little kid again. Oftentimes during those days I reflect and ponder the last year. I've written many of my diary entries, poems, and songs around that time—a time when I often used to find the strength that kept me going. This particular Christmas I needed to find the courage to finish what I had begun, to close the last door left open. I had to let Mom know how I felt about what she had done to me. I had to walk away from my past, from her, forever. I had to make her feel some of the shame and the embarrassment I'd carried around with me. I had to see sorrow in her face. I wanted her to feel bad, I wanted her to weep.

Yes, I wanted my revenge. But I also wanted to forgive her.

ONCE I WAS ON my own and comfortable with my life I was able to begin the process of healing and forgiveness. The healing was subject to time and patience. The forgiveness took a conscious effort. I hadn't spoken to Mom in over four years. I felt that now was the time to find a place to bury the hatchet somewhere other than in each other's forehead.

It was 1991. As Thanksgiving approached, I was spending most of my time managing a new restaurant in Colonial Heights, Virginia. I had a new apartment, new clothes, new friends, and a new life. I had no family around, and I had grown accustomed to being away from the Nichols family. Some people, finding themselves alone, get depressed during the holidays. Holidays never bothered me; it wasn't difficult being alone now. Once I got over the Nichols family moving to Minnesota, I had no reason to feel sorry for myself. I was supporting myself and I was comfortable. It felt good to be able to take pride in myself.

I had to close that last door—on my relationship with Mom—once and for all. Having not spoken to her in many years, it wasn't like there was any relationship to mend. I just wanted peace of mind.

When I returned home from the restaurant, I liked to settle down by the fire. The warmth and the smell of the burning wood were soothing. The comfort I derived from this was well worth the time spent. Often I would arrive home after closing time, past 2 A.M., and sit and keep the fire going until sunrise. More times than not I would sit up just thinking. Many of my journal entries were completed during those nights sitting in front of the fire.

Once Thanksgiving was over and the Christmas rush was in full swing, I worked as much as I could. The time passed quickly. I had started to write down the events of the last year that stuck in my mind. I was also going over the last several years' worth of journals and pondering the feelings and thoughts I'd expressed in them.

I found a shoe box of old photos. Some of them helped me to recall the emotions and feelings I'd written about. But many were simply too difficult to recall and ended up in the fire.

Several of the episodes that had meant something to me at the time I had since forgotten about. The time when Steve Nichols was helping me move out of the house I rented on Rosegill Road in Richmond was one of them.

Steve was about sixteen then, and hadn't yet received his driver's license. We had loaded a couch with various boxes and lamps on top in the back of a pickup truck to move to my new rental. As Steve started to drive the truck out of the driveway, the couch slid slowly right out the back, landing on the driveway with every item that we'd piled on top of it in place. Nothing was broken—nothing had even moved.

The look on Steve's face was priceless: a combination of horror and amusement. It was like a scene from a silent comedy. We split our sides laughing, then reloaded the truck and went on our way. Steve and I had always had fun. We enjoyed laughing over stupid things like that.

One of the journals contained a lot of entries about Steve and Wendy. Reading through these was guaranteed to remind me of some experience that I was thankful to be a part of, something I could smile about. I recalled the time when Wendy had been looking forward to her sixteenth birthday. She had planned it out with military precision. When the time came for her friends to arrive, John, Darlene, and I slipped into the background, allowing her the space and the freedom she needed to be herself. It was interesting to see her beginning to move away from dependence on her parents toward something like independence. It was nice to be a part of that time in her life. I had never had a sixteenth birthday party—or a fifteenth, or a fourth, or any birthday party for that matter, until I moved in with the Nichols family.

As I sat there by the fire I found myself actually laughing out loud. The warmth of the fire and the comfort I felt at this moment were special to me. I found a blanket from the bedroom and made another cup of chocolate. I couldn't get over how different I now was from how I used to be. I remembered the time I would sleep at Mesa Park in Sandy City, Utah, stoned out of my mind, cold, lifeless, and ashamed. Now I liked myself.

The memories I revisited that night made me sad and yet happy.

When I turned twenty-three, Heather Nichols was ten. She gave me a pepper shaker for my birthday. Heather always made fun of the fact that I used pepper on my food like it was going out of style. She was so funny about it—she thought it was the best gift she had ever given anyone. She may have been right.

John and Darlene produced a cake and ice cream, and we all sat around the dinner table and I opened my presents. It was a little odd being that old and celebrating my birthday like that. But it was a family event, and that was fine with me. It was the first birthday cake I could ever remember.

I had finally found what I had been looking for, a family that cared and shared in each other's life and parents that looked out for me and allowed me to grow at my own pace. John, Darlene, and the kids helped me in ways that I would never be able to repay.

———

As I read more and more of what I had written over the years, I became more convinced than ever that my life really was now on the right track. All I needed to complete the task I had undertaken was to let Mom know how I felt.

I decided to send her a letter, outlining my life over the last several years. I would tell her about my accomplishments as well as the failures. I wanted to show her that I had overcome my past, and was now reconciling myself to it as best I could.

Putting pen to paper could be difficult. Each night I would draft another letter, then tear it up or toss it into the fire. Writing in my journal was different—it was private, and no one would ever see it. This was harder because it was going to be read by the one person I wanted to completely forget about.

But the letters never really said what I wanted them to. I couldn't find the words that would describe the anger and the disappointment. I was especially angry over the fact that she had managed to forget about everything. Things she had done or things she hadn't done—it was all the same: unfair. More than that, it was nothing less than a crime that she was able to find peace with herself when several of her children were still dealing with the mental and emotional carnage. It was unfair that she was able to move on in her life when I was still struggling with all the baggage she had left me with. The years and years I'd spent being so self-destructive and abusing drugs were a direct result of what she had done to me, I felt sure.

I wanted to take all the feelings of guilt and shame that I had dragged around with me for over fifteen years and un-load them on her—then close the door, walk away, and never look back. I desperately wanted to sling all the blame for my shortcomings and my problems onto her. And I was consumed with the need to find the right words to do just that. In draft after draft I set down my fears, my anger, and my resentment, and yet I still wasn't able to express it all to my satisfaction. I wanted my words to make it incontrovert-ibly clear, once and for all, that she was at least partially to blame for my shortcomings, that hers was the responsibility for all of my issues over the years.

———————

Just before Christmas I was walking in Colonial Heights mall in Richmond, watching the kids and their parents. The interaction between them was just like I had always imagined the holiday spirit to be: families together, searching for treasures for dads, moms, brothers, and sisters. I somehow expected all the parents to be about the same age as Mom, and yet she was now in her early sixties. I watched younger parents about the same age as I was, interacting with their young kids. I thought about the joy and fun of shopping as a little boy.

Then I began to ponder. My own childhood was horrific, no doubt about that. And Mom should have been put in prison—no doubt about that, either. But I did have a few memories of better times. And here were people my own age and their families, getting on with their lives. Perhaps I had kept the anger and pain buried so deep and for so long that it was *continuing* to consume me, preventing me from *ever* growing up. If so, that alone was evidence that I was nowhere near ready to be a husband or father, let alone a dad like John. Was I so hung up with chasing after my lost childhood ghosts that I could never really move on?

Maybe it wasn't all *her fault. I guess I couldn't really blame my recklessness, my impulse to feed off the drug craze, entirely on her.*

Now that I was really thinking about it, perhaps I couldn't really blame her for anything that I did after a certain point in my life. Sure, when I was five and she was an outrageous alcoholic, abusive and all but possessed, that was *all* her. *But what about when I was seventeen and living in Hawaii, thousands of miles away—could I really blame any of that on her?*

Or what about my experience in the military—could I blame any of that on her?

As the people surged out of Sears and JCPenney and passed by me in the mall, I began to wonder again exactly when it was that I became responsible for myself. And about what had changed me from the little abused kid to the not so little and self-abusive teenager. There had to be something that I'd missed all these years.

Back home, it was all I could think about.

Have I been guilty all this time?

Did I really do this to myself?

When did I lose my dependency on Mom?

Maybe that's *the key to it*, I thought.

Maybe, the moment I became independent of her, I became dependent on myself. Once I'd lost the emotional and spiritual connection between mother and son—such as it was—that was when I was on my own.

When did I lose that connection?

When was it that I just said to myself: "That's it!"?

There had to be some event when I either changed my-self, or someone changed me. I lay in bed wondering—until I fell asleep, I guess.

With the new dawn came the answer I was looking for. Sometime in my sleep, somewhere deep down in my sub-conscious, I had recalled the moment of change. The words repeated themselves over and over again in my head:

Like a dog, like a dog, like a dog.

I knew exactly what the memory was and where it was from.

Just before I ratted David out to Mom for the last time, she'd treated me like a dog. She even went so far as to make me lick the floor—like a dog. It was at that moment that I concluded I was no longer a person, let alone her son. I had been severed from the family, from society, and now I was severed from myself. I was, from that moment, an animal. She had broken me and I knew it.

In that moment I changed. In that moment Mom changed me. She lost her son, and I lost my mother. We were separated, permanently.

Once I recalled that horrific and overcharged memory, I realized that the information I needed had been there all along.

Why didn't I see it before?

Why didn't I understand it then?

Now I understood, and now I could write the Christmas letter. It flowed like water, the emotions and the memories. I felt finally able to express my thoughts and feelings in an honest and factual way to her. It seemed to take no time at all to get everything down. I read it over and over again to make sure that it was just right.

I had done it. I had let go of the pain, the fear, and the tears of more than twenty years, and now I was comfortable with Mom. I knew who she was back then, and I knew just who she had regressed into, and it didn't matter to me. She had no effect on me anymore.

It was over, and I was the one who had ended it. I had taken the better path. I could stand tall in the knowledge that I was the one who had made the crucial move. I had reconciled with *her*.

I was free. Finally I was free.

16

THE CHRISTMAS LETTER

It said everything I wanted to say. It said everything I ever needed to say to her. The Christmas letter was my way of finally letting go and accepting the fact that I was an adult now. "Mom" was no more. All I'd had to do was let her know how I felt. It took a long time to find the right words in my head to express what I wanted to say, but once I'd found them and started putting them down on paper, they flowed like water from a tap. When I was done, it was like I was born again. An entire new life ahead of me.

But I made one mistake: I waited too long.

AFTER USING UP SEVERAL dozens of sheets of paper and spending many nights in front of the fire, I did it. I wrote the letter to Mom that would allow me to walk away a man. That Christmas Day I gave myself the most meaningful gift possible. The letter was dated December 25, 1991:

Roerva,

After stumbling through life, and with the scars I carry that few people have ever seen, I finally understand. I understand who you are. But more importantly I understand who I am.

All through my life you reminded me that I was worthless, small, meek, and shameful. At one point I knew you were right. I was exactly what you raised me to be.

For over twenty years I spent most of my time hiding and running away from the only thing you ever gave me: horrific memories.

You taught me the meaning of fear.

Just so you know—as a teenager I was reckless, suicidal, and a drug addict. Most of what you told the neighbors was true. I was "bad news." But not any longer.

You gave me the ability to hide almost anything from anybody.

Now I don't have to hide anything. I am who I am.

One of the only conversations I ever had with you that meant anything to me, you told me you "can't remember."

It's incredible that you don't recall the damage and the scars you caused me for years.

But now I know different. I believe that you have buried those emotions, those horrible and frightening emotions, so deep that even you can't recall them anymore.

Well—here I am giving you a gift; a gift that only I can give you.

I give to you a part of me. It's the part that I carried around for so long. It's the part of my life that was so heavy, at times I couldn't bear it any longer.

I give you the memories that I carried with me, the memories of the fear and pain that you inflicted on children that happened to be your own.

The scars and the damage you caused are permanent and have taken years' worth of tears and pain to even begin to understand. Today—Christmas Day—it hit me and I now understand. I used to feel pity and remorse for you. Now I feel shame for you.

It's a miracle in itself that I feel anything for you. You have taught me the meaning of silent tears. You have taught me the meaning of pity and shame. Overall you have forced me to find myself in that place where those memories are kept. It took more effort than anything I have ever done on this earth.

The only two things of any value that you have ever given me are the desire and ability to express myself in writing, and my life. Other than that, there is nothing I can say I am thankful for from you.

Today I'm free.

Today I am letting you go.

I'm free of the guilt—the fear and the shame.

You, too, have, in your own way, become free of it all as well. You have the luxury of being out of your mind, liter-

ally. I wish I could close by saying: I love you. But I can't—
I don't.

I do have to thank you.

You have made me stronger. You have given me a chance to experience life in a way that few others on this earth have experienced. You allowed me to become tempered in that fire you kept alive. The fire of fear and pain that children too small to defend themselves fear to find.

I am stronger than you can imagine.

You gave me the desire to be better. I know I can be a better parent than you were capable of. I have to be.

For so long I wondered if I even should be a father, fearing that I carry your disease—but I now know that it was you all along. Not some illness—that came later.

Thank you for giving me life.

Thank you for the opportunity to decide for myself if it was worth living or not.

Your son,
Richard

17

OVER?

It was done. It was over. And I was the one that had ended it. I put the letter in an envelope and placed it on my dresser. I wanted to hold on to the sheer pride of it for just a few days, before I mailed it out. I never expected a reply and left off the return address—I didn't want to take the chance that she would once again twist the closure I now felt into some meaningless shame.

I never got what I wanted. She beat me to it.

WORK WENT ON AS USUAL, and I felt like I had the world by the tail. Being alone during the holidays really didn't matter—everything was in place. Christmas became New Year's and I hung on to the freedom I now felt, and I hung on to the letter.

I decided that I would take it down to the post office that Saturday. I would let go of everything it signified as I dropped it into the mailbox. It was going to be a small ceremony, just for me.

But just before that fateful day came, while I was at work, it happened. The bartender at the restaurant came over to me. There was a phone call for me, he said.

"Can you take a message?" I asked.

"It's your brother, Ross."

I froze. I knew that it was something bad. Instantly, I recalled the moment I realized that Dad had died and that I'd known it even before the phone rang. This time it was different. I couldn't imagine what it was; I just knew it was something bad.

"Hello," I said, with my heart in my throat.

"Richard, it's Ross. Listen, Mom died last night."

The silence hung on the phone line. Each of us knew that the other was still on the line, but for a moment not a word was spoken. He gave me the information I needed about the funeral arrangements, we exchanged a few words, then I hung up. Immediately, all of those emotions I thought I'd buried came rushing to the surface. I felt anger, pain, shame, fear—and yes, sorrow. I was crushed.

On the flight out all I could think about was the letter I now carried in my pocket. Somehow, I thought in my confusion, I could still get it to her and she would understand.

It wasn't until I saw her in the county morgue that I believed it, that it really hit me. We were gathered there together in silence, all my brothers and my grandmother. It had been almost twenty years since all of the boys and Mom were in the same room. It was the first time I had seen David's face in almost as many years.

She had no makeup on—not that she ever wore any. The silence was perfect.

I'm not sure what I'd expected. I simply stood there. I felt my pocket and the letter it held; I thought about what I wanted to say to her. Before we left the morgue, I handed the letter to the mortician who'd showed us to the viewing room.

"When you cremate her, will you place this in with her?" I asked.

It was over. Once and for all. I'd said my piece, and she now had her own peace.

As I walked out I knew that she would have my letter for all time, all eternity. She would now carry what I couldn't carry any longer.

I was free.

It was over.

AFTERWORD

Several years ago when I started to compile and assemble the memoirs and journal entries that evolved into *A Brother's Journey* and *A Teenager's Journey*, the intention was that they would simply sit on my shelf as a reminder of where I came from and what I had been through. But as the work developed it became clear that reliving the memories was just too difficult for me to cope with alone. So with the help of my wife, who showed immense patience and such a strong desire to understand, my writing became not only a way for me to become reconciled with my life, but also a therapy.

In the beginning, as I read through my diaries, I would write as though the thoughts and feelings were reborn from the fire. The emotions that came to the surface from that place that was once so deep and dark reminded me just how far apart two beings could be, Mom and me, living our separate lives in separate places, and yet sharing one past. At one point I couldn't read my own work without choking on the emotions that the memories churned up.

As always time heals the wounds, and in the end I was able to read and understand. I understood that the time I'd spent carrying it all around like a stone around my neck was lost time, and that to continue doing so was futile. There was no reason to hold it in, no point in continuing to carefully manage the constant emotional eruptions. I'd spent most of my young life "high" and separated from my emotions. I'd lost more than pride during those years; I'd lost the chance to be a teenager. It was such a waste for me to have lived such a destructive life at that age. Why continue on that path?

Once I understood that the aim of assembling my memories should be to heal, not just to remind me of the past or record it, I was free. I also knew that others needed the same chance—the chance to let it all go and yet at the same time to assimilate it. As the work progressed and took shape, it became clear to me that here was an opportunity to share with others that have been there, and perhaps advance their healing process, too. What really happened here was something I never knew possible—it was indeed a process of healing and closure.

Without the help and support of my wife Joanne, I'm sure I would have found it too difficult and not seen the real value in sharing the experience. She helped me understand and adjust. Once the secrets were shared and the thoughts and feelings reopened, Joanne and I became even closer. Without her faith in me, there wouldn't have been closure.

And that is the most important part of this process—being able to walk away and still look forward to life.

My wife took a vagabond and made me whole.

She took a child and made me a man.

She helped me come to terms with what I kept for so long below the surface.

Now I can say: *It's finally over.*

I know that someday my own children will read this work and find it difficult to comprehend that I lived that way for so long. Currently, they have no idea of the events that took place so long ago. They couldn't possibly imagine the emotions, the feelings, and the heartache, and that's the way it should be.

One day, when they know what happened to their father, I hope they will understand.

It's not what we once were that matters, or what we thought of ourselves before today. What really matters is that we know who we are now, and what we can accomplish. We are all greater than the sum of our emotions. Whatever our age, at some level we are all children. Never let go of that.

To all the things that each of us has been through, and all that we'll ever feel, hear, learn, or experience, there must be a purpose. There must be a reason why we're born into certain families, find certain spouses, and progress through life the way we do.

We are all looking for the answer to the undying question: Why am I here? For me I found the answer in the least likely place I looked: deep within myself.

If we were to take all of our emotions, thoughts, feelings, and experiences and hold them in our hand, they would be like a single grain of sand. When we realize the magnitude of all the grains of sand in the world, we get but a glimpse of the potential experiences we are destined to embrace.

Once we understand our true potential and when we go through life a day at a time, we recognize that there is nearly nothing that we cannot accomplish or endure, if we but remember from whence we came.

There is nothing greater on this earth than the value of just one child's soul.

Joanne,

Thanks for allowing me to be a kid. Now I know what it means to see time stand still before me. I know that you're the reason I came on this earth and lived the life I have.

You're my reward.

AUTHOR'S NOTE

With the love of my family and the support of my wife, I have completed a part of me that was left unfinished for so long. Sharing this story with the world has helped me immensely. It has also made me realize that there are other relationships that I must attend to, those other characters spoken of that were at some time, like me, held captive.

My journey has come to a threshold that I must now choose to cross. I speak of that place where all those emotions were once held silent, that place where others were in their own way left behind. Those siblings find it just as difficult to recall, remember, and embrace those days of long ago. I have a new journey: a journey I should have taken twenty years ago, a journey of recalculation and repair. Only this journey isn't just for myself, it's for those who really understand.

None of this would have been possible without Wendy, Steve, Heidi, Heather, Adam, Amy, and of course John and

Darlene. Those teenage years were the hardest and yet the most meaningful.

My advice to my readers:

Surround yourself with true friends who care and who can share with you. Don't be afraid to let go of the child and find the young adult. You're never really alone.

SILENT TEARS

When you look into the eyes of the future you
often see the past.
It's only when a wife is concerned for
the silent tears you shed
and that she cannot see, that it's discussed.

In that discussion you try to explain the difference
between silent tears and tears of silence.

The difference is as large as the imagination of a child.

Tears of silence are the tears of joy in watching
the future grow before your very eyes.

They are the tears of joy—healing the heartache
and watching for the choices between right and wrong and
teaching the difference.

Silent tears are those that are not seen by man or woman,
they are the tears created and seen only by a child.

Eventually you try to explain to your partner that these
tears not seen are for the flashes of the past,

The flashes that occur from time to time
without provocation.

They are the emotions that are raised when you find
yourself disciplining a child,
wondering—have I crossed that line?

The conversations that you never had that would change
the meaning of tears forever are yet to be born.

The conversations that would bring voice to those silent
tears are the monsters under the bed.

The words that would wake the dead are
better left to those poor souls buried without tears,
be they tears of silence or silent tears.

One day a man decides that the monsters under the bed
are real and very much alive.

They live in his mind as a memory
reborn when he closes his eyes to sleep.

As time goes on they cause the ability to sleep with his eyes
open, instilling fear in the one that sleeps next to him.

She wonders what could have happened to a
man that would cause such a trait.

She sits wondering what events have occurred that would
bring a man to such a fear of the dark.

A fear of the sounds that only a mother makes as she walks
into his bedroom.

Somehow the sleep that is required by this man is
replaced with midnight awakenings in a shout of fear.

The need to stay awake overpowers the need
to sleep—again the body and the mind have adjusted.

Notwithstanding this, a son's love for his mother is
stronger than the willpower required to keep
the silent tears unheard.

Mom—I love you.

And more than that, I forgive you.

Please forgive me for giving voice to the once silent tears.

Now, like you, please, please let the monsters
under the bed be put to rest.
Your son—Richard

CHILD ABUSE
PREVENTION RESOURCES

The National Exchange Club Foundation

The National Exchange Club Foundation is committed to making a difference in the lives of children, families, and our communities through its national project, the prevention of child abuse. The NEC Foundation's most successful method of countering abuse is by working directly with parents through the parent aid program. The NEC Foundation coordinates a nationwide network of nearly one hundred Exchange Club Child Abuse Prevention Centers that utilize the parent aid program and provide support to families at risk for abuse.

The National Exchange Club
Child Abuse Prevention Services Department
3050 Central Avenue
Toledo, OH 43606-1700
Phone: 800-924-2643 (800-XCHANGE)
Fax: 419-535-1989
Web site: www.preventchildabuse.com
Contact: www.preventchildabuse.com/contact.htm

For the past several years, the blue ribbon has been widely recognized as a national symbol of child abuse awareness. This movement began in the spring of 1989, when a concerned grandmother, Bonnie Finney of Norfolk, Virginia, took a stand against child abuse after the death of her grandson. She tied a symbolic blue ribbon to her van as a signal to the community of her personal commitment to involve everyone in the battle to stop child abuse. Bonnie's own grandson was a tragic, young victim, and his death gave her the strength to encourage others to help in the fight against child abuse and neglect. The spirit of her blue ribbon grew, and it inspired a statewide community-based effort to join forces in this tragic battle.

Today, the blue ribbon symbolizes the more than 3.2 million abused children reported each year to Child Protective Services (CPS) throughout the United States.

During the month of April, Child Abuse Prevention Month, nearly 1,100 Exchange Clubs and NEC Child Abuse Prevention Centers conduct a blue ribbon campaign in their communities across America.

For more information, contact:
Richard B. Pelzer
124 Long Pond Road, Suite 8
Plymouth, MA 02360
508-746-6080
www.richardpelzer.com

B
PELZER

Pelzer, Richard B.

A teenager's
journey.

$23.95

DATE			

5 -16 -06